THE CANON OF THE BIBLE.

THE
CANON OF THE BIBLE:

ITS FORMATION, HISTORY,
AND FLUCTUATIONS.

BY

SAMUEL DAVIDSON, D.D.

OF HALLE, AND LL.D.

THIRD EDITION, REVISED AND ENLARGED.

WIPF & STOCK · Eugene, Oregon

Wipf and Stock Publishers
199 W 8th Ave, Suite 3
Eugene, OR 97401

The Canon of the Bible
Its Formation, History and Fluctuations
By Davidson, Samuel
ISBN 13: 978-1-55635-795-4
Publication date 1/9/2008
Previously published by C. Kegan Paul & Co., 1880

PREFACE.

THE substance of the present work was written towards the close of the year 1875 for the new edition of the "Encyclopædia Britannica." Having been abridged and mutilated, contrary to the author's wishes, before its publication there, he resolved to print it entire. With that view it has undergone repeated revision with enlargement in different parts, and been made as complete as the limits of an essay appeared to allow. As nothing of importance has been knowingly omitted, the writer hopes it will be found a comprehensive summary of all that concerns the formation and history of the Bible canon. The place occupied by it was vacant. No English book reflecting the processes or results of recent criticism, gives an account of the canon in both Testaments. Articles and essays upon the subject there are; but their standpoint is usually apologetic not scientific, traditional rather than impartial, unreasonably conservative without being critical. The topic is weighty, involving the consideration of great questions, such as the inspiration, authenticity, authority, and age of the Scriptures. The author has tried to handle it fairly, founding his statements on such evidence as seemed convincing, and condensing them into a moderate compass. If the reader wishes to know the evidence, he may find it in the writer's Introductions to the Old and New Testaments, where the separate books of Scripture are discussed; and in the late treatises of other critics. While his expositions are capable of expansion, it is believed that they will not be easily shaken. He commends the work to the attention of all who have an interest in the progress of theology, and are seeking a foundation for their faith less precarious than books however venerable.

It has not been the writer's purpose to chronicle phases of opinion, or to refute what he believes to be error in the newest hypotheses about the age, authority, and composition of the books. His aim has been rather to set forth the most correct view of the questions involved in a history of the canon, whether it be more or less recent. Some may think that the latest or most current account of such questions is the best; but that is not his opinion. Hence the fashionable belief that much of the Pentateuch, the Book of Leviticus wholly, with large parts of Exodus and Numbers, in a word, that all the laws relating to divine worship with most of the chronological tables or statistics, belong to Ezra, who is metamorphosed in fact into the first Elohist, is unnoticed. Hence also the earliest gospel is not declared to be Mark's. Neither has the author ventured to place the fourth gospel at the end of the first century, as Ewald and Weitzsäcker do, after the manner of the old critics; or with Keim so early as 110-115 A.D.

Many evince a restless anxiety to find something novel; and to depart from well-established conclusions for the sake of originality. This shews a morbid state of mind. Amid the feverish outlook for discoveries and the slight regard for what is safe, conservatism is a commendable thing. Some again desire to return, as far as they can, to orthodoxy, finding between that extreme and rationalism a middle way which offers a resting-place to faith. The numerous changes which criticism presents are not a symptom of soundness. The writer is far indeed from thinking that every question connected with the books of Scripture is finally settled; but the majority undoubtedly are, though several already fixed by great scholars continue to be opened up afresh. He does not profess to adopt the phase of criticism which is fashionable at the moment; it is enough to state what approves itself to his judgment, and to hold it fast amid the contrarieties of conjecture or the cravings of curiosity. Present excrescences or aberrations of belief will have their day and disappear. Large portions of the Pentateuch will cease to be consigned to a post-exile time, and the gospels of Matthew and Luke will again be counted the chief sources of Mark's. It will also be acknowledged that the first as it now exists, is of much later origin than the fall of Jerusalem. Nor will there be so great anxiety to show that Justin Martyr was acquainted with the fourth gospel, and owed his Logos-doctrine chiefly to it. The difference of ten or twenty years in the date of a gospel will not be considered of essential importance in estimating its character.

The present edition has been revised throughout and several parts re-written. The author hopes that it will be found still more worthy of the favour with which the first was received.

May 1878.

CONTENTS.

	PAGE
CHAPTER I.	
INTRODUCTORY,	1
CHAPTER II.	
THE OLD TESTAMENT CANON FROM ITS BEGINNING TO ITS CLOSE,	10
CHAPTER III.	
THE SAMARITAN AND ALEXANDRIAN CANONS,	81
CHAPTER IV.	
NUMBER AND ORDER OF THE SEPARATE BOOKS,	92
CHAPTER V.	
USE OF THE OLD TESTAMENT BY THE FIRST CHRISTIAN WRITERS, AND THE FATHERS TILL THE TIME OF ORIGEN,	97
CHAPTER VI.	
THE NEW TESTAMENT CANON IN THE FIRST THREE CENTURIES,	108

CHAPTER VII.

THE BIBLE CANON FROM THE FOURTH CENTURY TO THE REFORMATION, ... 173

CHAPTER VIII.

ORDER OF THE NEW TESTAMENT BOOKS, . . 221

CHAPTER IX.

SUMMARY OF THE SUBJECT, ... 231

CHAPTER X.

THE CANON IN THE CONFESSIONS OF DIFFERENT CHURCHES, ... 240

CHAPTER XI.

THE CANON FROM SEMLER TO THE PRESENT TIME, WITH REFLECTIONS ON ITS READJUSTMENT, . 247

THE CANON OF THE BIBLE.

CHAPTER I.

INTRODUCTORY.

As introductory to the following dissertation, I shall explain and define certain terms that frequently occur in it, especially *canon, apocryphal, ecclesiastical*, and the like. A right apprehension of these will make the observations advanced respecting the canon and its formation plainer. The words have not been taken in the same sense by all, a fact that obscures their sense. They have been employed more or less vaguely by different writers. Varying ideas have been attached to them.

The Greek original of *canon*[1] means primarily a straight rod or pole; and metaphorically, what

---
[1] κανών.

serves to keep a thing upright or straight, a *rule*.
In the New Testament it occurs in Gal. vi. 16
and 2 Cor. x. 13, 15, 16, signifying in the former,
a measure; in the latter, what is measured, a *district*.
But we have now to do with its ecclesiastical use. There are three opinions as to the origin
of its application to the writings used by the
church. According to Toland, Whiston, Semler,
Baur, and others, the word had originally the
sense of *list* or *catalogue* of books publicly read
in Christian assemblies. Others, as Steiner, suppose that since the Alexandrian grammarians
applied it to collections of Old Greek authors
as *models* of excellence or *classics*, it meant
classical (canonical) *writings*. According to a
third opinion, the term included from the first
the idea of a regulating principle. This is the
more probable, because the same idea lies in the
New Testament use of the noun, and pervades
its applications in the language of the early
Fathers down to the time of Constantine, as

Credner has shown.[1] The "canon of the church" in the Clementine homilies;[2] the "ecclesiastical canon,"[3] and "the canon of the truth," in Clement and Irenæus;[4] the "canon" of the faith in Polycrates,[5] the *regula fidei* of Tertullian,[6] and the *libri regulares* of Origen,[7] imply a *normative principle*. But we cannot assent to Credner's view of the Greek word for *canon* being an abbreviation of "Scriptures of canon,"[8] equivalent to *Scripturæ legis* in Diocletian's Act[9]—a view too artificial, and unsanctioned by usage.

It is true that the word *canon* was employed by Greek writers in the sense of a mere *list;*

[1] *Zur Geschichte des Kanons*, pp. 3-68.
[2] Clement. Hom. *ap. Coteler.*, vol. i. p. 608.
[3] *Stromata*, vi. 15, p. 803, ed. Potter.
[4] *Adv. Hæres.*, i. 95.
[5] *Ap.* Euseb. H. E., v. 24.
[6] *De præscript. Hæreticorum*, chs. 12, 13.
[7] *Comment. in Mat.* iii. p. 916; ed. Delarue.
[8] γραφαὶ κανόνος.
[9] *Monumenta vetera ad Donatistarum historiam pertinentia*, ed. Dupin, p. 168.

but when it was transferred to the Scripture books, it included the idea of a regulative and normal power—a list of books forming a rule or law, because the newly-formed Catholic Church required a standard of appeal in opposition to the Gnostics with their arbitrary use of sacred writings. There is a lack of evidence on behalf of its use before the books of the New Testament had been paralleled with those of the Old in authority and inspiration.

The earliest example of its application to a catalogue of the Old or New Testament books occurs in the Latin translation of Origen's homily on Joshua, where the original seems to have been "canon."[1] The word itself is certainly in Amphilochius,[2] as well as in Jerome,[3] and Rufinus.[4] As the Latin translation of Origen

[1] κανών.

[2] At the end of the *Iambi ad Seleucum*, on the books of the New Testament, he adds, οὗτος ἀψευδέστατος κανὼν ἂν εἴη τῶν θεοπνεύστων γραφῶν.

[3] *Prologus galeatus* in ii. Reg.

[4] *Expos. in Symb. Apost.*, 37, p. 374, ed. Migne.

has *canonicus* and *canonizatus*, we infer that he used "canonical,"[1] opposed as it is to *apocryphus* or *secretus*. The first occurrence of "canonical" is in the fifty-ninth canon of the Council of Laodicea, where it is contrasted with two other Greek words.[2] "*Canonized* books,"[3] is first used in Athanasius's 39th festal epistle.[4] The kind of rule which the earliest fathers attributed to the Scriptures can only be conjectured; it is certain that they believed the Old Testament books to be a *divine* and *infallible guide*. But the New Testament was not so considered till towards the close of the second century when the conception of a Catholic Church was realized. The latter collection was not called *Scripture*, or put on a par with the Old Testament as

[1] κανονικός. [2] ἰδιωτικός and ἀκανόνιστος. [3] Κανονιζόμενα.
[4] After the word is added, καὶ παραδοθέντα, πιστευθέντα τὲ θεῖα εἶναι. *Opp.*, vol. i. p. 962, ed. Benedict. The festal or passover letters of the Alexandrian bishops were pastorals addressed to the church in Egypt, at the approach of the yearly festival of Easter. It was natural that they should have some authority there.

sacred and *inspired*, till the time of Theophilus of Antioch (about 180 A.D.) Hence Irenæus applies the epithets *divine* and *perfect* to the Scriptures; and Clement of Alexandria calls them *inspired*.

When distinctions were made among the Biblical writings other words[1] were employed, synonymous with "canonised."[2] The canon was thus a catalogue of writings forming a rule of truth, sacred, divine, revealed by God for the instruction of men. The rule was perfect for its purpose.

The word apocryphal[3] is used in various senses, which it is difficult to trace chronologically. Apocryphal books are,—

1st, Such as contain *secret* or *mysterious* things, books of the higher wisdom. It is thus applied to the Apocalypse by Gregory of Nyssa.[4] Akin to this is the second meaning.

---

[1] Such as ἐνδιάθηκα, ὡρισμένα. [2] κανονιζόμενα or κεκανονισμένα.
[3] ἀπόκρυφος. [4] *Orat. de Ordin.*, vol. ii. p. 44.

2nd, Such as were *kept secret* or withdrawn from public use. In this sense the word corresponds to the Hebrew *ganuz*.[1] So Origen speaking of the story of Susanna. The opposite of this is *read in public*,[2] a word employed by Eusebius.[3]

3rd, It was used of the secret books of the heretics by Clement[4] and Origen,[5] with the accessory idea of *spurious, pseudepigraphical*,[6] in opposition to the canonical writings of the Catholic Church. The book of Enoch and similar productions were so characterized.[7]

4th, Jerome applied it to the books in the

---

[1] גָּנֻז. The Jews applied the word *genuzim* to books withdrawn from public use, whose contents were thought to be out of harmony with the doctrinal or moral views of Judaism when the canon was closed. See Fürst's *Der Kanon des alten Testaments*, p. 127, note; and Geiger's *Urschrift*, p. 201.

[2] δεδημοσιευμένα.

[3] H. E. II. 23, III. 3-16.

[4] *Stromata*, lib. iii. p. 1134, ed. Migne.

[5] *Prolog. ad Cant.*, *opp.*, vol. iii. p. 36.

[6] νόθος, ψευδεπίγραφος.

[7] See Suicer's *Thesaurus, s. v.*

Septuagint which are absent from the Hebrew canon, *i.e.*, to the books which were *read* in the church, the *ecclesiastical* ones[1] occupying a rank next to the canonical. In doing so he had respect to the corresponding Hebrew epithet. This was a misuse of the word *apocryphal*, which had a prejudicial effect on the character of the books in after-times.[2] The word, which he did not employ in an injurious sense, was adopted from him by Protestants after the Reformation, who gave it perhaps a sharper distinction than he intended, so as to imply a contrast somewhat disparaging to writings which were publicly read in many churches and put beside the canonical ones by distinguished fathers. The Lutherans have adhered to Jerome's meaning longer than the Reformed; but the decree of the Council of Trent had

[1] Βιβλία ἀναγινωσκόμενα, libri ecclesiastici.

[2] In his epistle to Laeta he uses the epithet in its customary sense, of books unauthentic, not proceeding from the authors whose names they bear. *Opp.*, vol. i. p. 877, ed. Migne.

some effect on both. The contrast between the canonical and apocryphal writings was carried to its utmost length by the Westminster divines, who asserted that the former are inspired, the latter not.

CHAPTER II.

THE OLD TESTAMENT CANON FROM ITS BEGINNING TO ITS CLOSE.

THE first important part of the Old Testament put together as a whole was the Pentateuch, or rather, the five books of Moses and Joshua. This was preceded by smaller documents, which one or more redactors embodied in it. The earliest things committed to writing were probably *the ten words* proceeding from Moses himself, afterwards enlarged into the ten commandments which exist at present in two recensions (Exod. xx., Deut. v.) It is true that we have the oldest form of the decalogue from the Jehovist not the Elohist; but that is no valid objection against the antiquity of the nucleus out of which it arose. It is also probable that several legal and ceremonial enactments belong, if not to Moses himself, at least to his time; as also the Elohistic list of stations in Numbers xxxiii. To the same time belongs the song of Miriam in Exodus xv., probably consisting of a few lines at first, and subsequently enlarged; with a triumphal ode over the fall of Heshbon (Numbers xxi. 27-30). The little poetical piece in Numbers xxi. 17, 18, afterwards misunderstood and so taken literally, is post-Mosaic.

During the unsettled times of Joshua and the Judges there could have been comparatively little writing. The song of Deborah appeared, full of poetic force and fire. The period of the early kings was characterized not only by a remarkable development of the Hebrew people and their consolidation into a national state, but by fresh literary activity. Laws were written out for the guidance of priests and people; and the political organization of the rapidly growing nation was promoted by poetical productions in which spiritual life expressed its aspirations. Schools of prophets were instituted by Samuel, whose literary efforts tended to purify the worship. David was an accomplished poet, whose psalms are composed in lofty strains; and Solomon may have written a few odes. The building of the temple, and the arrangements connected with its worship, contributed materially to a written legislation.

During this early and flourishing period, appeared the book of the Wars of Jehovah,[1] a heroic anthology, celebrating warlike deeds; and the book of Jashar,[2] also poetical. Jehoshaphat is mentioned as court-annalist to David and Solomon.[3] Above all, the Elohists now appeared, the first of whom, in the reign of Saul, was author of annals beginning at the earliest

[1] Num. xxi. 14. [2] Joshua x. 12, 13; 2 Sam. i. 18.
[3] 2 Sam. viii. 16; 1 Kings iv. 3.

time which were distinguished by genealogical and chronological details as well as systematic minuteness, by archaic simplicity, and by legal prescriptions more theoretical than practical. The long genealogical registers with an artificial chronology and a statement of the years of men's lives, the dry narratives, the precise accounts of the gradual enlargement of divine laws, the copious description of the tabernacle and the institution of divine worship, are wearisome, though pervaded by a theoretic interest which looks at every thing from a legal point of view. A second or junior Elohist was less methodical and more fragmentary, supplying additional information, furnishing new theocratic details, and setting forth the relation of Israel to heathen nations and to God. In contrast with his predecessor, he has great beauty of description, which is exemplified in the account of Isaac's sacrifice and the history of Joseph; in picturesque and graphic narratives interspersed with few reflections. His parallels to the later writer commonly called the Jehovist, are numerous. The third author, who lived in the time of Uzziah, though more mythological than the Elohists, was less formal. His standpoint is prophetic. The third document incorporated with the Elohistic ones formed an important part of the whole, exhibiting a vividness which the first lacked; with descriptions of persons and things from another stand-point. The Jehovist belonged to the northern kingdom; the Elohists were of Judah.

The state of the nation after Rehoboam was unfavourable to literature. When the people were threatened and attacked by other nations, divided among themselves in worship and all higher interests, rent by conflicting parties, the theocratic principle which was the true bond of union could not assert itself with effect. The people were corrupt; their religious life debased. The example of the kings was usually prejudicial to political healthiness. Contact with foreigners as well as with the older inhabitants of the land, hindered progress. In these circumstances the prophets were the true reformers, the advocates of political liberty, expositors of the principles that give life and stability to a nation. In Judah, Joel wrote prophetic discourses; in Israel, Amos and Hosea. Now, too, a redactor put together the Elohistic and Jehovistic documents, making various changes in them, adding throughout sentences and words that seemed desirable, and suppressing what was unsuited to his taste. Several psalm-writers enriched the national literature after David. Learned men at the court of Hezekiah recast and enlarged (Proverbs xxv.—xxix.) the national proverbs, which bore Solomon's name because the nucleus of an older collection belonged to that monarch. These literary courtiers were not prophets, but rather scribes. The book of Job was written, with the exception of Elihu's later discourses which were not inserted in it till after the return from Babylon; and Deuteronomy, with Joshua, was added to the preceding collection in the reign of Manasseh. The gifted author of Deuteronomy, who was evidently imbued with the prophetic spirit, completed the Pentateuch, *i.e.*, the five books of Moses and Joshua, revising the Elohist-Jehovistic work, and making various additions or alterations. He did the same thing to the historical books of Judges, Samuel, and Kings; which received from him their present form. Immediately before and during the exile there were numerous authors and compilers. New psalms appeared, more or less national in spirit. Ezekiel, Jeremiah and others prophesied; especially an unknown seer who described the present condition of the people, predicting their coming glories and renovated worship in strains of far-reaching import.[1] This great prophet

[1] Isaiah xl.-lxvi.

expected the regeneration of the nation from the pious portion of it, the prophets in particular, not from a kingly Messiah as Isaiah did; for the hopes resting on rulers out of David's house had been disappointed. His aspirations turned to spiritual means. He was not merely an enthusiastic seer with comprehensive glance, but also a practical philosopher who set forth the doctrine of the innocent suffering for the guilty; differing therein from Ezekiel's theory of individual reward and punishment in the present world—a theory out of harmony with the circumstances of actual life. The very misfortunes of the nation, and the signs of their return, excited within the nobler spirits hopes of a brighter future, in which the flourishing reign of David should be surpassed by the universal worship of Jehovah. In consequence of their outward condition, the prophets of the exile were usually writers, like Ezekiel, not public speakers; and their announcement of glad tidings could only be transmitted privately from person to person. This explains in part the oblivion into which their names fell; so that the author or redactor of Jeremiah l., li.; the authors of chapters xiii.-xiv. 23, xxi. 1-10, xxiv.-xxvii., xxxiv., xxxv., inserted in Isaiah; and, above all, the Babylonian Isaiah, whom Hitzig improbably identifies with the high-priest Joshua, are unknown. After the return from Babylon the literary spirit manifested itself in the prophets of the restoration— Haggai, Zechariah, and Malachi—who wrote to recall their countrymen to a sense of religious duties; though their ideas were borrowed in part from older prophets of more original genius. The book of Esther appeared, to make the observance of the purim feast, which was of Persian origin, more general in Palestine. The large historical work comprising the books of Ezra, Nehemiah, and Chronicles, was compiled partly out of materials written by Ezra and

Nehemiah, partly out of older historical records which formed a portion of the national literature. Several temple-psalms were also composed; a part of the present book of Proverbs; Ecclesiastes, whose tone and language betray its late origin; and Jonah, whose diction puts its date after the Babylonian captivity. The Maccabean age called forth the book of Daniel and various psalms. In addition to new productions there was an inclination to collect former documents. To Zechariah's authentic prophecies were added the earlier ones contained in chapters ix.—xiv.; and the Psalms were gradually brought together, being made up into divisions at different times; the first and second divisions proceeding from one redactor, the third from another, the fourth and fifth from a still later. Various writings besides their own were grouped around the names of earlier prophets, as was the case with Isaiah and Jeremiah.

The literature is more indebted for its best

constituents to the prophetic than to the priestly order, because the prophets were preachers of repentance and righteousness whose great aim was to make Israel a Jehovah-worshipping nation to the exclusion of other gods. Their utterances were essentially ethical and religious; their pictures of the future subjective and ideal. There was silently elaborated in their schools a spiritual monotheism, over against the crude polytheism of the people generally—a theocratic ideal inadequately apprehended by gross and sensuous Israel—Jehovism simple and sublime amid a sacerdotal worship which left the heart impure while cleansing the hands. Instead of taking their stand upon the law, with its rules of worship, its ceremonial precepts and penalties against transgressors, the prophets set themselves above it, speaking slightingly of the forms and customs which the people took for the whole of religion. To the view of such as were prepared to receive a faith that looked for its realisation to the future, they helped to create a millennium, in which the worship of Jehovah alone should become the basis of a universal religion for humanity. In addition to the prophetic literature proper, they wrote historical works also. How superior this literature is to the priestly appears from a comparison of the Kings and Chronicles. The subjective underlies the one; the objective distinguishes the other. Faith in Jehovah, clothed, it may be in sensible or historical forms, characterises the one; reference of an outward order to a divine source, the other. The sanctity of a people under the government of a righteous God, is the object of the one; the sanctity of institutions, that of the other. Even when the prophets wrote history, *the facts* are subordinate to *the belief*. Subjective purposes coloured their representation of real events.

To them we are indebted for the Messianic

idea, the hope of a better time in which their high ideal of the theocracy should be realised. With such belief in the future, with pious aspirations enlivening their patriotism, did they comfort and encourage their countrymen. The hope, general or indefinite at first, was afterwards attached to the house of David, out of which a restorer of the theocracy was expected, a king pre-eminent in righteousness, and marvellously gifted. It was not merely a political but a religious hope, implying the thorough purification of the nation, the extinction of idolatry, the general spread and triumph of true religion. The pious wishes of the prophets, often repeated, became a sort of doctrine, and contributed to sustain the failing spirit of the people. The indefinite idea of a golden age was commoner than that of a personal prince who should reign in equity and peace. Neither was part of the national faith, like the law, or the doctrine of sacrifice; and but a few of the prophets portrayed a king in their description of the period of ideal prosperity.

The man who first gave public sanction to a portion of the national literature was Ezra, who laid the foundation of a canon. He was the leader in restoring the theocracy after the exile, "a ready scribe in the law of Moses, who had prepared his heart to seek the law of the Lord and to teach in Israel statutes and judgments." As we are told that he brought the book of the law of Moses before the congregation and read it publicly, the idea naturally arises that he was the final redactor of the Pentateuch, separating it from the historical work consisting of Joshua and the subsequent writings, of which it formed the commencement. Such was the first canon given to the Jewish Church after its reconstruction—ready for temple service as well as synagogue use. Henceforward the Mosaic book became an authoritative guide in spiritual, ecclesiastical, and civil matters, as we infer from various passages in Ezra and Nehemiah and from the chronicler's own statements in the book bearing his name. The doings of Ezra with regard to the Scriptures are deduced not only from what we read of him in the Biblical book that bears his name, but also from the legend in the fourth book of Esdras,[1] where it is related that he dictated by inspiration to five ready writers ninety-four books; the first twenty-four of which he was ordered to publish openly that the worthy and unworthy might read, but reserved the last seventy for the wise. Though the twenty-four books of the Old Testament cannot be attributed to him, the fact that he copied and wrote portions need not be questioned. He edited *the law*, making the first canon or collection of books, and giving it an authority which it had not before. Talmudic accounts associate with him the men of the great

---

[1] Chap. xiv. 23-50, &c. See Hilgenfeld's *Messias Judæorum*, p. 107.

synagogue. It is true that they are legendary, but there is a foundation of fact beneath the fanciful superstructure. As to Ezra's treatment of the Pentateuch, or his specific mode of redaction, we are left for the most part to conjecture. Yet it is safe to affirm that he added;—making new precepts and practices either in place of or beside older ones. Some things he removed as unsuited to the altered circumstances of the people; others he modified. He threw back later enactments into earlier times. It is difficult to discover all the parts that betray his hand. Some elaborate priestly details show his authorship most clearly. If his hand be not visible in Leviticus chap. xvii.—xxvi.; a writer not far removed from his time is observable; Ezekiel or some other. It is clear that some of the portion (xxv. 19—22; xxvi. 3—45) is much later than the Elohists, and belongs to the exile or post-exile period. But great difficulty attaches to the separation of the sources here used; even after Kayser's acute handling of them. It is also perceptible from Ezekiel xx. 25, 26, that the clause in Exodus xiii. 15, " but all the firstborn of my children I redeem," was added after the exile, since the prophet shews his unacquaintance with it. The statute that all which openeth the womb should be burnt in sacrifice to Jehovah, appeared inhuman not only to Ezekiel, but to Ezra or his associates in re-editing the law; and therefore the clause about the redemption of every firstborn male was subjoined. Ezra, a second Moses in the eyes of the later Jews, did not scruple to refer to Moses what was of recent origin, and to deal freely with the national literature. Such was the first canon—that of Ezra the priest and scribe.

The origin of the great synagogue is noticed in Ezra x. 16, and described more particularly in Nehemiah viii.-x., the members being apparently enumerated in x. 1-27; at least the

Megila Jer. (i. 5) and Midrash Ruth (§ 3) speak of an assembly of eighty-five elders, who are probably found in the last passage. One name, however, is wanting, for only eighty-four are given; and as Ezra is not mentioned among them, the conjecture of Krochmal that it has dropped out of x. 9 may be allowed. Another tradition gives the number as one hundred and twenty, which may be got by adding the "chief of the fathers" enumerated in Ezra viii. 1-14 to the hundred and two heads of families in Ezra ii. 2-58. Whether the number was the same at the commencement as afterwards is uncertain. Late Jewish writers, however, such as Abarbanel, Abraham ben David, Ben Maimun, &c., speak as if it consisted of the larger number at the beginning; and have no scruple in pronouncing Ezra president, rather than Nehemiah.[1]

[1] See Buxtorf's *Tiberias*, chap. x., p. 88, &c.; and Herzfeld's *Geschichte des Volkes Israel*, vol. i. p. 380, &c. Zwölfter Excursus.

The oldest extra-biblical mention of the synagogue is in the Mishnic treatise *Pirke Aboth*, where it is said, "Moses received the law from Mount Sinai, and delivered it to Joshua, Joshua to the elders, the elders to the prophets, and the prophets delivered it to the men of the great synagogue. These last spake these words: "Be slow in judgment; appoint many disciples; make a hedge for the law"[1] In the Talmudic *Baba Bathra*, their biblical doings are described: "Moses wrote his book, the section about Balaam and Job. Joshua wrote his book and eight verses of the law. Samuel wrote his book and Judges and Ruth. David wrote the book of Psalms *by* (?)[2] ten elders, by Adam the first man, by Melchizedek, by Abraham, by Moses, by He-

---

[1] Chapter i.

[2] על ידי. Does this mean *for*, *instead of*, as Bloch understands it? Waehner inserts, to fill up the sense, "some of which, however, were composed by;" but this is far-fetched. See *Antiquitates Ebræorum*, p. 13.

man, by Jeduthun, by Asaph, and the three sons of Korah. Jeremiah wrote his book, the books of Kings and Lamentations. Hezekiah and his friends wrote Isaiah, Proverbs, Canticles, and Coheleth; the men of the great synagogue, Ezekiel, the twelve prophets, Daniel and Esther. Ezra wrote his own book and the genealogies of Chronicles down to himself."[1] This passage has its obscurities. What is meant by the verb *write?*[2] Does it mean *composition* and then something else; the former in the first part of the passage, and *editing* in the second? Rashi explains it of *composition* throughout, which introduces absurdity. The most obvious interpretation is that which understands the verb of *writing* in one place, and *editing* in the second. But it is improbable that the author should have used the same word in different senses, in one and the same

[1] Fol. 15, 1.   [2] כָּתַב.

passage, Bloch[1] understands it of *copying* or *writing out*, a sense that suits the procedure of the men of the great synagogue in regard to Ezekiel, the twelve prophets, &c., but is inapplicable to Moses, Joshua, Samuel, David, Jeremiah, &c. It is probable enough that the synagogue scribes put into their present form and made the first authorised copies of the works specified. The Boraitha, however, is not clear, and may only express the opinion of a private individual in a confused way. Simon the Just is said to have belonged to the remnants of the synagogue. As Ezra is called "a ready scribe," and his labours in connection with the law were important, he may have organised a body of literary men who should work in harmony, attending, among other things, to the collection and preservation of the national literature; or they may have

[1] *Studien zur Geschichte der Sammlung der althebräischen Literatur*, p. 127, &c.

been an association of patriotic men who voluntarily rallied round the heads of the new state, to support them in their fundamental reforms. The company of scribes mentioned in 1 Maccabees does not probably relate to it.[1] A succession of priests and scribes, excited at first by the reforming zeal of one whom later Jews looked upon as a second Moses, laboured in one department of literary work till the corporation ceased to exist soon after if not in the time of Simon, *i.e.*, from about 445 B.C. till about 200; for we identify the Simon celebrated in Sirach l. 1-26 with Simon II., son of the high-priest Onias II., B.C. 221-202; not with Simon I., son and successor of the high-priest Onias I., B.C. 310-291. Josephus's opinion, indeed, is contrary; but leading Jewish scholars, such as Zunz, Herzfeld, Krochmal, Derenbourg, Jost, and Bloch differ from him.

[1] vii. 12, συναγωγὴ γραμματέων, not ἡ συναγωγή.

To the great synagogue must be referred the compilation of the second canon, containing Joshua, Judges with Ruth, Samuel, Kings, Isaiah, Jeremiah with Lamentations, Ezekiel and the twelve minor prophets. It was not completed prior to 300 B.C., because the book of Jonah was not written before. This work may be called a historical parable composed for a didactic purpose, giving a milder, larger view of Jehovah's favour than the orthodox one that excluded the Gentiles. Ruth, containing an idyllic story with an unfinished genealogy attached meant to glorify the house of David, and presenting a kindred spirit towards a people uniformly hated, was appended to Judges; but was subsequently transferred to the third canon. It was written immediately after the return from the Babylonian captivity; for the Chaldaising language points to this date, notwithstanding the supposed archaisms discovered in it by some. In like manner, the

Lamentations, originally added to Jeremiah, were afterwards put into the later or third canon. Joshua, which had been separated from the five books of Moses with which it was closely joined at first, formed, with the other historical portion (Judges, Samuel, Kings), the proper continuation of Ezra's canon. The prophets included the three greater and twelve minor. With Isaiah's authentic oracles were incorporated the last twenty-seven chapters, belonging for the most part to an anonymous prophet of the exile, besides several late pieces inserted in the first thirty-nine chapters. Men of prophetic gifts wrote in the name of distinguished prophets, and put their productions with those of the latter, or adapted and wrote them over after their own fashion. The fiftieth and fifty-first chapters of Jeremiah shew such over-writing. To Zechariah's authentic oracles were attached chapters ix.-xiv., themselves made up of two parts (ix.-xi., xii.-xiv.) belonging to different times and authors prior to the destruction of the Jewish state by the Babylonians.

The character of the synagogue's proceedings in regard to the books of Scripture can only be deduced from the conduct of Ezra himself, as well as the prevailing views and wants of the times. The scribes who began with Ezra, seeing how he acted, would naturally follow his example, not hesitating to revise the text *in substance* as well as form.[1] They did not refrain from changing what had been written, or from inserting fresh matter. Some of their novelties can be discerned even in the Pentateuch. Their chief work, however, related to the *form* of the text. They put into a proper

---

[1] That the Scribes always adhered to the prohibition to write no religious laws and ordinances cannot be held, even in the face of the Talmudic saying, כותב הילכות כשורף תורה (writers of Halacoth are like a burner of the law). This may apply to the late scribes or bookmen, not to the earlier. The greater part of Geiger's *Urschrift* is based on the opposite idea. As the reverence for former scholars increased, the Talmudic saying might be accepted. See *Temura*, 14 b.

form and state the text of the writings they studied, perceiving less need for revising the *matter*. What they did was in good faith, with honest intention.

The prophetic canon ended with Malachi's oracles. And it was made sometime after he prophesied, because the general consciousness that the function ceased with him required a considerable period for its growth. The fact that it included Jonah and Ruth brings the completion after 300 B.C., as already stated. There are no definite allusions to it till the second century B.C. Daniel speaks of a passage in Jeremiah being in "the books" or "writings;"[1] and the prologue of Jesus Sirach presupposes its formation. Such was the second canon, which had been made up gradually (444-290 B.C.)

Another view of the collection in question has been taken by various scholars. Accord-

[1] Chapter ix. 2.

ing to a passage in the second book of Maccabees, the second canon originated with Nehemiah, who "gathered together the acts of the kings and the prophets and (psalms) of David, and the epistles of the kings concerning the holy gifts."[1] These words are obscure. They occur in a letter purporting to be sent by the Sanhedrim at Jerusalem to the Jews in Egypt, which contains apocryphal things; a letter which assigns to Nehemiah the merit of various arrangements rather belonging to Ezra. It is difficult to understand the meaning of "the epistles of the kings concerning the offerings." If they were the documents of heathen or Persian kings favourable to the rebuilding of Jerusalem and its temple, would they not have been rejected from a collection of sacred books belonging to the chosen people? They might perhaps have been adopted had they

[1] Chapter ii. 13.

been interwoven with the holy books themselves, like portions of Ezra and Nehemiah; but they could not have formed a distinct part of the national literature, because they were foreign and heathen. Again, "the psalms of David" cannot have existed in the time of Nehemiah, if the phrase includes the whole collection. It may perhaps refer to the first three divisions of the book, as Herzfeld thinks; but these contain many odes which are not David's; while earlier ones belong to the last two divisions of the Psalm-book. In like manner, "the prophets" could not all have belonged to this canon; neither Malachi, who was later, nor Jonah. The account will not bear strict examination, and must be pronounced apocryphal. Nehemiah was a statesman, not a priest or scribe; a politician, not a literary man. It is true that he may have had assistants, or committed the work to competent hands; but this is conjectural. The account of his supposed canon hardly commends itself by inherent truthfulness or probability, though it is accepted by Ewald and Bleek.

When the great synagogue ceased, there was an interval during which it is not clear whether the sacred books were neglected, except by private individuals; or whether they were studied, copied, and collected by a body of scribes. Perhaps the scribes and elders of the Hasmonæan time were active at intervals in this department. The institution of a senate by Judas Maccabaeus is supposed to be favoured by 2 Maccabees (chapter i. 10—ii. 18); but the passage furnishes poor evidence of the thing. Judas is there made to write to Egypt in the year of the Seleucidae 188, though he died thirty-six years before, *i.e.*, 152. Other places have been added as corroborative, viz., 2 Maccab. iv. 44, xi. 27; 1 Maccab. vii. 33. Some go so far as to state that Jose ben Joeser was appointed its first president at that time. The Midrash in Bereshith Rabba (§ 65) makes him one of the sixty Hassidim who were treacherously murdered by Alcimus; but this is neither in the first book of the Maccabees (chapter vii.) nor in Josephus,[1] and must be pronounced conjectural. It is impossible to fix the exact date of Jose ben Joeser in the Hasmonean period. Pirke Aboth leaves it indefinite. Jonathan, Judas Maccabaeus's successor, when writing to the Lacedaemonians, speaks of the *gerusia* or senate as well as *the people* of the Jews; whence we learn that the body existed as early as the time of Judas.[2] Again, Demetrius writes to Simon, as also to *the elders* and *nation* of the Jews.[3] After Jonathan and Simon, it may have been suspended for a while, in consequence of the persecution

---

[1] Antiq., xii. 10, 1.
[2] Josephus's Antiq., xiii. 5, 8; 1 Maccab., xii. 35.
[3] 1 Maccab., xiii. 36.

and anarchy prevailing in Judea; till the great Sanhedrim at Jerusalem succeeded it, under Hyrcanus I. Though the traces of a senate in the Maccabaean epoch are slight, the Talmud countenances its existence.[1] We believe that it was earlier than Judas Maccabaeus. Of its constitution nothing is known; but it was probably aristocratic. The Hasmonean prince would naturally exert a commanding influence over it. The great synagogue had been a kind of democratic council, consisting of scribes, doctors or teachers, and priests.[2] Like their predecessors of the great synagogue, the Hasmonæan elders revised the text freely, putting into it explanatory or corrective additions, which were not always improvements. The way in which they used the book of Esther, employing it as a medium of Halachite prescription, shews a treatment involving little

---

[1] Sota, 24 a.   [2] מבינים, Nehemiah viii. 3.

idea of sacredness attaching to the Hagiographa.

We are aware that the existence of this body is liable to doubt, and that the expressions belonging to it in Jewish books, whether elders or *gerusia*, have been applied to the great synagogue or to the Sanhedrim at Jerusalem, or even to the elders of any little town or hamlet; but it is difficult to explain all on that hypothesis, without attributing confusion to the places where they occur. If the body in question be not allowed, an interval of about sixty years elapsed between the great synagogue and the Sanhedrim, during which the hagiographical writings were comparatively neglected, though literary activity did not cease. No authoritative association, at least, dealt with them. This is improbable. It is true that we read of no distinguished teachers in the interval, except Antigonus of Socho, disciple of Simon the Just; but the silence can hardly weigh against a reasonable presumption. One thing is clear, viz., that Antigonus did not reach down to the time of the first pair that presided over the Sanhedrim.

The contents of the third canon, *i.e.*, Psalms, Proverbs, Job, Canticles, Ecclesiastes, Esther, Daniel, Ezra, Nehemiah, Chronicles, the formation of which we assign to the Hasmonæan *gerusia*, were multifarious, differing widely from one another in age, character, and value—poetical, prophetic, didactic, historical. Such as seemed worthy of preservation, though they had not been included in the second canon, were gathered together during the space of an hundred and fifty years. The oldest part consisted of psalms supposed to belong to David. The first psalm, which contains within itself traces of late authorship, was prefixed as an introduction to the whole collection now put into the third canon. Next to the Psalms were Proverbs, Job, Canticles, which, though non-prophetic and probably excluded on that account from the second canon, must have existed before the exile. Enriched with the latest additions, they survived the national disasters, and claimed a place next to the Psalms. They were but a portion of the literature current in and after the 5th century B.C., as may be inferred from the epilogue to Ecclesiastes, and the Wisdom of Sirach. The historical work compiled by the chronicle-writer was separated, Ezra being put first as the most important part and referring also to the church of the 6th and 5th centuries whose history had not been written. The Chronicles themselves were placed last, being considered of less value than the first part, as they contained the summary of a period already described, though with numerous adaptations to post-exile times. The youngest portion consisted of the book of Daniel, not written till the Maccabean period (between 170 and 160 B.C.);[1] and probably of several Psalms (44, 60, 74, 75, 76, 79, 80, 83, 89, 110, 118) which were inserted in different places of the collection to make the whole number 150. These late odes savour of the Maccabean time; and are fitly illustrated by the history given in the first book of Maccabees. The list continued open; dominated by no stringent principle of selection, and with a character somewhat indefinite. It was called *c'tubim*,

[1] Talmudic tradition, which attributes the redaction of the book to the men of the great synagogue who are said to have acted under the influence of the divine spirit, separates the three apocryphal pieces from the rest; but this arose from the desire of discountenancing the idea that the work consists of romance and legend. Such later tradition took curious ways of justifying the canonicity of Daniel and the redaction of it by the great synagogue, *ex gr.*, the assumption that the second part arose out of a series of unconnected *Megiloth* which were not reduced to chronological order. Still the Midrash maintains that Daniel, or the person writing in his name, was no prophet, like Haggai, Zechariah, and Malachi, but a man of visions, an *apocalyptist*. It was a general belief, that *visions* had come into the place of *prophecy* when the book appeared. The Greek translation could not have been long after the original, because it is used in the First Book of Maccabees.

i.e., writings ;[1] a general epithet suited to the contents.

Several books put into the third canon,—as Job, Proverbs, the greater number of the Psalms, &c.,—existed when the second was made. But the latter collection was pre-eminently *prophetic;* and it was that idea of the origin and contents of the books in it which regulated its extent. Bloch's supposition that the parts of the third collection then existing were not looked upon as

---

The interval between the Hebrew and the Greek was inconsiderable. The translator not only departed from, but added to, the original, inserting such important pieces as the Prayer of Azarias, the Song of the Three Children, the History of Susanna, and that of Bel and the Dragon. Whether any of these had been written before is uncertain. Most of the traditions they embody were probably reduced to writing by the translator, and presented in his peculiar style. The assertion, that Josephus was unacquainted with these additions is hazardous, since the way in which he speaks of Daniel's fame (Antiq. x. 11, 7), and especially of *the books* he wrote (τὰ βιβλία), supposes some relation to them. Elsewhere he speaks of *one book* (x. 10, 4 ; xi. 8, 5), where he may have thought of the canonical part.

[1] כְּתוּבִים, translated by the Greek ἁγιόγραφα, hagiographa.

holy, but merely as productions embodying human wisdom, and were therefore excluded, is improbable. We do not think that an alteration of opinion about them in the course of a century or more, by which they became divine and holy instead of human, is a satisfactory explanation. The Psalms of David and the book of Job must have been as highly esteemed in the period of the great synagogue's existence as they were at a later time. Other considerations besides the divinity and holiness of books contributed to their introduction into a canon. Ecclesiastes was taken into the third collection because it was attributed to Solomon. The Song of Songs was understood allegorically,— a fact which, in addition to its supposed Solomonic authorship, determined its adoption. And even after their canonical reception, whether by the great synagogue or another body, the character of books was canvassed. It was so with Ecclesiastes, in spite of the *supposed* sanction it got from the great synagogue contained in the epilogue, added, as some think, by that body to attest the sacredness of the book.[1]

While the third canon was being made, the soferim, as the successors of the prophets, were active as before; and though interpretation was their chief duty, they must have revised and corrected the sacred books to some extent. We need not hesitate to allow that they sometimes arranged parts, and even added matter of their own. In the time of the canon's entire preparation, they and the priests, with writers and scholars generally, redacted the national literature, excluding or sanctioning such portions of it as they thought fit.

---

[1] It has been thought that the phrase בעלי אספות in the ninth verse alludes to the great council or synagogue. This conjecture is plausible on various grounds. The reasons for attributing the epilogue to a later time than the writer of the book appear to be stronger than those assigning it to the original author. The 13th and 14th verses in particular, are unlike Coheleth.

At this time appeared the present five-fold partition of the Psalms, preceded as it had been by other divisions, the last of which was very similar to the one that became final. Several inscriptions and historical notices were prefixed. The inscriptions, however, belong to very different times, their historical parts being usually older than the musical; and date from the first collection to the period of the Hasmonean college, when the final redaction of the entire Psalter took place. Those in the first three books existed at the time when the latter were made up; those in the last two were prefixed partly at the time when the collections themselves were made, and partly in the Maccabean age. How often they are out of harmony with the poems themselves, needs no remark. They are both traditional and conjectural.

The earliest attestation of the third canon is that of the prologue to Jesus Sirach (130 B.C.), where not only *the law and the prophets* are specified, but "the other books of the fathers," or "the rest of the books."¹ No information is given as to its extent, or the particular books included. They may have been for the most part the same as the present ones. The passage does not show that the third list was closed. The better writings of the fathers, such as tended to learning and wisdom, are not excluded by the definite article. In like manner, neither Philo nor the New Testament gives exact information as to the contents of the division in question. Indeed, several books, Canticles, Esther, Ecclesiastes, are unnoticed in the latter. The argument drawn from Matthew xxiii. 35, that the Chronicles were then the last book of the canon, is inconclusive; as the Zechariah there named was probably different from the Zechariah in

¹ τὰ ἄλλα πάτρια βιβλία; τὰ λοιπὰ τῶν βιβλίων. The younger Sirach does not use γραφαί, which would have been a proper translation of *c'tubim*. Does not this ἄλλα imply the non-application of the specific title *c'tubim* to the hagiographa at that time, and therefore the idea that the third canon was still open?

2 Chronicles xxiv. None of these witnesses proves that the third canon was finally closed.

A more definite testimony respecting the canon is given by Josephus towards the end of the first century A.D. "For we have not an innumerable multitude of books among us, ... but only twenty-two books, which contain the records of all the past times.; which are justly believed to be divine. And of them five belong to Moses. . . . . But as to the time from the death of Moses till the reign of Artaxerxes king of Persia, the prophets who were after Moses wrote down what was done in their times in thirteen books. The remaining four books contain hymns to God and precepts for the conduct of human life. It is true our history has been written since Artaxerxes very particularly, but has not been esteemed of the like authority with the former by our forefathers, because there has not been an exact succession of prophets since that time: and how firmly we have given credit to these books of our own nation is evident by what we do; for during so many ages as have already passed, no one has been so bold as either to add anything to them, to take anything from them, or to make any change in them; but it has become natural to all Jews immediately and from their very birth, to esteem these books to contain divine doctrines, and to persist in them, and if occasion be, willingly to die for them."[1] This list agrees with our present canon, showing that the Palestinian Jews were tolerably unanimous as to the extent of the collection. The thirteen prophets include Job; the four lyric and moral books are Psalms, Proverbs, Ecclesiastes and Canticles.

It is not likely that the Hasmonæan senate had a long existence. It was replaced by the Sanhedrim, a more definite and state institution,

[1] *Contra Apion*, i. 8.

intended as a counter-balance to the influence of the Hasmonæan princes. The notices of the latter reach no further back than Hyrcanus I., *i.e.*, about 135 B.C.[1] Josephus speaks of it under Hyrcanus II.[2] It cannot be referred to an earlier period than Hyrcanus I. Frankel[3] indeed finds a notice of it in 2 Chronicles xix. 8, 11; but the account there is indistinct, and refers to the great synagogue. The compiler having no certain information about what was long past, transfers the origin of the court he speaks of to Jehoshaphat, in order to glorify the house of David. It is impossible to date the Sanhedrim, with Frankel, in the Grecian era, in which case it must have been dissolved during the Maccabean insurrection, and after-

---

[1] In Maaser Sheni, Sota 24. 1, the duumvirate or suggòth, consisting of the president, Nasi, and vice-president, Ab-beth-din, are referred to Hyrcanus's creation. Zunz affirms that it originated in the time of Simon, son of Mattathias, 142 B.C.

[2] Antiq., xiv., 9.

[3] *Der gerichtliche Beweis*, p. 68.

wards reconstructed; it was not constituted till about 130 B.C. Whether it was modelled after the great synagogue or the Hasmonæan senate, is uncertain. The idea of it may have been suggested by the latter rather than the former, for its basis was aristocratic. The Hasmonæan *gerusia* must have been less formal and definite than the Sanhedrim; though the latter arose before the family ceased to be in power, and differed materially from its predecessor. It continued from 130 B.C. till A.D. 180, surviving the terrible disasters of the nation.[1]

The closing of the third canon cannot be assigned, with Bloch, to the great synagogue. If the college ceased with or before Simon, *i.e.*, about 200-192, and the work of Daniel did not appear till about 170 B.C., twenty years at

[1] The Sanhedrim *properly so called* ceased under R. Judah I., Ha-Nasi, when the council of seventy members which sat at Sepphoris before his patriarchate, transferred its privileges to him, on his removal to that place. The court was then merged in the patriarch.

least intervened between the extinction of the great synagogue and Daniel's book. This holds good, whether we assume, with Krochmal, the synagogue's *redaction* of the work,—more correctly the putting together of the independent parts of which *it is said* to be composed; or equally so, if the taking of it into the canon as a book already completed be attributed to the same body. But we are unable to see that Krochmal's reasoning about the synagogue putting Daniel's work together and one of the members writing the book of Esther is probable.

In like manner, Maccabean psalms are adverse to the hypothesis that the great synagogue completed the third canon. In consequence of these late productions, it is impossible to assert that the men of the synagogue were the redactors of the Psalter as it is. It is true that the collection was made before the Chronicles and many other books of the hagiographical canon; but the *complète* Psalter did not appear till the Maccabean period. The canon, however, was not considered to be finally closed in the first century before and the next after Christ. There were doubts about some portions. The book of Ezekiel gave offence, because some of its statements seemed to contradict the law. Doubts about others were of a more serious nature; about Ecclesiastes, the Canticles, Esther, and the Proverbs. The first was impugned because it had contradictory passages and a heretical tendency; the second, because of its worldly and sensual tone; Esther for its want of religiousness; and Proverbs on account of inconsistencies. This scepticism went far to procure the exclusion of the suspected works from the canon, and their relegation to the class of the *genuzim*.[1] But it did not prevail. Hananiah, son of

---

[1] גְּנוּזִים literally *concealed, withdrawn from public use.*

Hezekiah, son of Garon, about 32 B.C., is said to have reconciled the contradictions and quieted the doubts.[1] But these traces of resistance to the fixity of the canon were not the last. They reappeared about A.D. 65, as we learn from the Talmud,[2] when the controversy turned mainly upon the canonicity of Ecclesiastes, which the school of Shammai, who had the majority, opposed; so that the book was probably excluded.[3] The question emerged again at a later synod at Jabneh or Jamnia, when R. Eleasar ben Asaria was chosen patriarch, and Gamaliel the second deposed. Here it was decided, not unanimously however, but by a majority of Hillelites, that Ecclesiastes and the Song of Songs "pollute the hands," *i.e.*, belong properly to the Hagiographa.[4] This was about

---

[1] See Fürst's *Der Kanon des alten Testaments, u.s.w.* pp. 147, 148.   [2] *Tract. Sabbat.* ch. i.

[3] Because of its profane spirit and Epicurean ideas; see Adoyot v. 3.   [4] Yadayim v. 3.

90 A.D.[1] Thus the question of the canonicity of certain books was discussed at two synods.

Passages in the Talmud have been adduced to shew that the Shammaite objections to the canonicity of Ecclesiastes " were overruled by the positive declaration from the 72 elders, *being a testimony anterior to the Christian era* that Coheleth is canonical;" but they do not support the opinion.[2] "The sages" referred to in the treatise Sabbat and elsewhere is a vague expression, resting apparently on no historic tradition—a mere opinion of comparatively late date. If it refer to the Jerusalem

[1] See Graetz's *Kohelet*, pp. 162, 163.

[2] The sages wished to pronounce Coheleth apocryphal, because its statements are contradictory. And why have they not declared it apocryphal? Because it begins with words of the law, and ends with words of the law, for it opens with the words " What advantage has man in all his labour wherewith he labours under the sun?" &c., &c.—Sabbat. 30 b.

So also in the Midrash: "The sages wished to pronounce Coheleth apocryphal," &c., &c.—Vayyikra rabba 161 b.

synod A.D. 65, the Hillelites were simply outnumbered there by the Shammaites. The matter was debated hastily, and determined for the time by a majority. But the synod at Jamnia consisted of 72 persons; and a passage in the treatise Yadayim refers to it.[1] The testimony of the 72 elders to whom R. Simeon ben Asai here alludes, so far from belonging to an ante-christian era, belongs to a date about 90 A.D. And the fact that the synod at Jamnia took up again a question already debated at Jerusalem A.D. 65, proves that no final settlement of the canon had taken place before. The canon was virtually settled at Jamnia, where was confirmed what R. Akiba said of the Canticles in his usual extravagant way: "No day in the whole history of the world is of so

---

[1] R. Simeon ben Asai said, "I have received it from the mouth of the 72 elders in the day that R. Eleasar ben Asaria was appointed elder, that the Song of Songs and Coheleth pollute the hands."—Yadayim v. 3.

much worth as the one in which the Song of Songs was given to Israel; for all the Scriptures are holy; but the Song of Songs is most holy."[1] As the Hagiographa were not read in public, with the exception of Esther, opinions of the Jewish rabbins might still differ about Canticles and Ecclesiastes, even after the synod of Jamnia.

In opposition to these remarks, it is strenuously argued by Bloch that neither the passage in the Mishnic treatise Yadayim, nor any other, refers to the *canonical character* of the books to which Jewish elders raised several objections. But his arguments are more vehement than valid. Anxious to assign the final settlement of the entire canon to an authoritative body like the great synagogue, he affirms that all parties were united in opinion about

[1] This language was based on a figurative interpretation of the Song. One who said, "Whoever reads such writings as Sirach and the later books loses all part in everlasting life," can have no weight. He outeroded the Palestinian tradition respecting the Jewish productions of later origin, which merely affirms that they "do not pollute the hands."—(*Toss. Yadayim*, c. 2.)

the time of Christ,—Assiim, Perushim, and Zeddukim; Shammaites and Hillelites. But it requires more than his ingenuity to explain away the meaning of Yadayim 3, 5, Adoyot v. 3, Sabbat 1. To what did such diversity of opinion relate, if not to the canonical character of the books? A specific answer to the question is not given by the learned writer,[1] who is too eager in his endeavour to attribute the settlement of the third canon to the great synagogue, and to smooth away all diversities of opinion about several books, after that time, as if none could afterwards question the authoritative settlement by that body. He will not even allow a wider canon to the Alexandrian Jews than that of their Palestinian brethren, though he cannot but admit that the former read and highly esteemed various apocryphal books because of their *theocratic* character. Surely the practical use of writings is an evi-

[1] *Studien zur Geschichte, u. s. w.*, p. 150, &c.

dence of their canonicity as strong as theoretical opinions.

The doubts about several books to which we have alluded, some of which Hananiah is said to have resolved in his old age, imply a diligent study of the national literature, if not a revision of the text; and the Tannaite college at Jabneh must have cared for the same things, as it had to deal with similar objections. After the last canon was made more than a century anterior to the Christian era, the text was not considered inviolate by the learned Jews; it received subsequent modifications and interpolations. The process of redaction had not ceased before the time of Christ. This was owing, among other causes, to the state of parties among the Jews, as well as the intrusion of Greek literature and culture, whose influence the Palestinian Jews themselves were not able altogether to withstand. When Jeremiah accused the Scribes of falsifying the law by their lying pen (viii. 8), it may be inferred that the same process took place afterwards; that offensive things were removed, and alterations made continuously down to the close of the canon, and even after. The corrections consisted of additions and changes of letters, being indicated in part by the most ancient versions and the traditions of the Jews themselves who often knew what stood in the text at first, and why it was altered. They are also indicated by the nature of the passage itself viewed in the light of the state of religion at the time. Here sober judgment must guard against unnecessary conjectures. Some changes are apparent, as the plural *oaks* in Genesis xiii. 18, xiv. 13, xviii. 1, Deuteronomy xi. 30, for the singular *oak*; and the plural *gods* in Exodus xxxii. 4 for the singular *god*. So 2 Sam. vii. 23, (comp. 1 Chron. xvii. 21, and LXX.);[1] and Deutero-

---

[1] Geiger's *Urschrift*, p. 288.

my xxxii. 8,[1] have been altered. Popper and Geiger have probably assumed too much correction on the part of the Scribes and others; though they have drawn attention to the subject in the spirit of original criticism.

Jewish literature began to degenerate after the captivity, and it continued to do so. It leant upon the past more and more, having an external and formal character with little of the living soul. The independence of their religious literature disappeared with the national independence of the Jews; and the genius of the people was too exclusive to receive much expansion from the spirit of nations with whom they came in contact. In such circumstances, amid the general consciousness of present misfortune which the hope of a brighter future could not dispel, and regretful retrospects of the past tinged with ideal splendour, the exact

[1] See De Goeje in the *Theologisch Tijdschriff Jaargang II.* (1868) p. 179, &c.

time of drawing a line between books that might be included in the third division of the canon must have been arbitrary. In the absence of a normal principle to determine selection, the productions were arbitrarily separated. Not that they were badly adjusted. On the contrary, the canon as a whole was settled wisely. Yet the critical spirit of learned Jews in the future could not be extinguished by anticipation. The canon was not really settled for all time by a synodical gathering at Jamnia; for Sirach was added to the Hagiographa by some rabbins about the beginning of the 4th century;[1] while Baruch circulated long in Hebrew, and was publicly read on the day of atonement in the third century, according to the Apostolic constitutions.[2] These two books were in high repute for a considerable time, possessing a kind of canonical credit

[1] Zunz's *Die gottesdienstlichen Vorträge*, pp. 101, 102.
[2] V. 20, p. 124, ed. Ueltzen.

even among the learned Jews of Palestine. Rab, Jochanan, Elasar, Rabba bar Mare, occasionally refer to Sirach in the way in which the *c'tubim* were quoted: the writer of Daniel used Baruch; and the translator of Jeremiah put it into Greek.

If it be asked on what principle books were admitted into the canon, a single answer does not suffice. One and the same criterion did not determine the process at all times. The leading principle with which the first canon-makers set out was to collect all the documents of Hebrew antiquity. This seems to have guided Ezra, if not the great synagogue after him. The nation, early imbued with the theocratic spirit and believing itself the chosen of God, was favourably inclined towards documents in which that standpoint was assumed. The legal and ethical were specially valued. The prophetic claimed a divine origin; the lyric or poetic touched and elevated the ideal faculty on which religion acts. But the leading principle which actuated Ezra and the great synagogue was gradually modified, amid the growing compass of the national literature and the consciousness that prophecy ceased with Malachi. When the latest part of the canon had to be selected from a literature almost contemporaneous, regard was had to such productions as resembled the old in spirit. Orthodoxy of contents was the dominant criterion. But this was a difficult thing, for various works really anonymous, though wearing the garb of old names and histories, were in existence, so that the boundary of the third part became uncertain and fluctuating.

The principle that actuated Ezra in making the first canon was a religious and patriotic one. From his treatment of the oldest law books we infer that he did not look upon them as inviolable. Venerable they were, and so far sacred; but neither perfect nor complete for all time.

In his view they were not unconditionally authoritative. Doubtless they had a high value as the productions of inspired lawgivers and men of a prophetic spirit; but the redaction to which he submitted them shows no superstitious reverence. With him *canonical* and *holy* were not identical. Nor does the idea of an *immediate, divine* authority appear to have dominated the mind of the great synagogue in the selection of books. Like Ezra, these scholars reverenced the productions of the prophets, poets, and historians to whom their countrymen were indebted in the past for religious or political progress; but they did not look upon them as the offspring of unerring wisdom. How could they, while witnessing repetitions and minor contradictions in the books collected?

The same remarks apply to the third canon. *Direct divinity* of origin was not the criterion which determined the reception of a book into it; but the character and authorship of the book. Did it breathe the old spirit, or proceed from one venerated for his wisdom? Was it like the old orthodox productions; or did it bear the name of one renowned for his piety and knowledge of divine things? The stamp of antiquity was necessary in a certain sense; but the theocratic spirit was the leading consideration. Ecclesiastes was admitted because it bore the name of Solomon; and Daniel's apocalyptic writings, because veiled under the name of an old prophet. New psalms were taken in because of their association with much older ones in the temple service. Yet the first book of Maccabees was excluded, though written in Hebrew. It is still more remarkable that Sirach was put among the external productions; but this was owing not so much to its recent origin, for it is older than the book of Daniel, as to its being an apparent echo of the Proverbs, and therefore unnecessary. Yet it was long after assigned to the Hagiographa, and quoted as such by several rabbis. Baruch was also left out, though it is as old as Daniel, if not older; and professes to have been written by Jeremiah's friend, in Babylon.

That redactors dealt freely with the text of the second and third canons especially, without a superstitious belief in its sacredness, is apparent from the double recension which existed when the Egyptian Jews translated the books into Greek. If the one that formed the basis of the Alexandrian version be less correct than the Palestinian in the majority of instances, it is still superior in many. The differences between them, often remarkable, prove that those who had most to do with the books did not guard them as they would have done had they thought them infallibly inspired. Palestinians and Alexandrians subjected the text to redaction; or had suffered it to fall into a state inconsistent with the assumption of its supernatural origin. At a much later period, the Masoretes reduced to one type all existing copies of their Scriptures, introducing an uniformity imperatively demanded in their opinion by multiplied discrepancies.

Whatever divine character the reflecting attributed to the canonical books, it must have amounted to the same thing as that assigned to human attributes and physical phenomena—a divinity resulting from the over-leaping of second causes, in the absence of inductive philosophy. Here the imperfection conditioned by the nature of the created cannot be hid. Yet the books may be truly said to have contained the word of God.

Of the three divisions, *the Law* or Pentateuch was most highly venerated by the Jews. It was the first translated into Greek; and in Philo's view was inspired in a way peculiar to itself. *The Prophets*, or second division, occupied a somewhat lower place in their estimation, but were read in the public services as the law had been before. The *c'tubim*, or third division, was not looked upon as equal to the Prophets in importance : only the five Megiloth were publicly read. The three parts of the collection present the three gradations of sanctity which the books assumed successively in Israelite estimation. A certain reverence was attached to all as soon as they were made canonical ; but the reverence was not of equal height, and the supposed authority was proportionally varied.[1] The consciousness of prophetism being extinct soon after the return from Babylon, was a genuine instinct. With the extinction of the Jewish state the religious spirit almost evaporated. The idealism which the old prophets proclaimed in contrast with the symbolic religion of the state gave place to forms and an attachment to the *written* law.

[1] Dillmann, in the *Jahrbücher für deutsche Theologie, dritter Band*, p. 422.

Religion came to be a thing of the understanding, the subject of learned treatment; and its essence was reduced to dogmas or precepts. Thus it ceased to be a spiritual element in which the heart had free scope for its highest aspirations. In addition to all, a foreign metaphysical theology, the Persian doctrine of spirits, was introduced, which seemed to enlarge the sphere of speculation, but really retarded the free exercise of the mind. As the external side of religion had been previously directed to the performance of good works, this externality was now determined by a written law. Even the prophetism that appeared after the restoration was little more than an echo of the past, falling in with an outward and written legalism. The literature of the people deteriorated in quality, and prophecy became *apocalypse*. In such circumstances the advent of a new man was needed to restore the free life of religion in higher power. Christ appeared in the fulness of time to do this effectually by proclaiming the divine Fatherhood, and founding a worship *in spirit and in truth*. Rising above the symbolic wrappings of the Mosaic religion, and relying upon the native power of the spirit itself, he shewed how man may mount up to the throne of God, adoring the Supreme without the intervention of temple, sacrifice, or ceremony.

When the three divisions were united, the ecclesiastical respect which had gathered round the law and the prophets from ancient times began to be transferred to the *c'tubim*. A belief in their sanctity increased apace in the 1st century before the Christian era, so that *sacredness* and *canonicity* were almost identical. The doubts of individuals, it is true, were still expressed respecting certain books of the *c'tubim*, but they had no perceptible effect upon the current opinion. The sanctity attaching to the last division as well as the others did not permit the total displacement of any part.

The passage in Josephus already quoted shows the state of the canon about A.D. 100. According to it, he considered it to have been closed at the time of Artaxerxes Longimanus, whom he identifies with the Ahasuerus of Esther, 464-424 B.C. The books were divine, so that none dared to add to, substract from, or alter them. To him the canon was something belonging to the venerable past, and inviolable. In other words, all the books were peculiarly sacred. Although we can scarcely think this to be his private opinion merely, it is probably expressed in exaggerated terms, and hardly tallies with his use of the third Esdras in preference to the canonical texts.[1] His authority, however, is small. Bloch's estimate of it is too high. It is utterly improbable that Josephus's opinion was universally held by the Jews in his day. His division of the books is peculiar: five Mosaic, thirteen

[1] In his *Antiq.*, x. 4, 5, and xi. 1-5.

historical, four containing religious songs and rules of life. It appears, indeed, that as he had the same twenty-two books we now have, Ruth was still attached to Judges, and Lamentations to Jeremiah; but his credit is not on a par with that of a Jew who adhered to his countrymen in the time of their calamity. He wrote for the Romans. One who believed that Esther was the youngest book in the canon, who looked upon Ecclesiastes as Solomon's, and Daniel as an exile production, cannot be a competent judge. In his time the historical sense of the book of Daniel was misapprehended; for after the Grecian dynasty had fallen without the fulfilment of the Messianic prophecy connected with it, the Roman empire was put into its place. Hence various allusions in The History of the Jewish Wars.[1] The passage in the Antiquities,[2] about Alexander the Great and

[1] iv. 6, sec. 3, and vi. 2, sec. 1.
[2] xi. 8, sec. 5.

the priests in the Temple at Jerusalem is apocryphal. In any case, Josephus does not furnish a genuine list of the canonical books any more than Philo. The Pharisaic view of his time is undoubtedly given, that the canon was then complete and sacred. The decision proceeded from that part of the nation who ruled both over school and people, and regained supremacy after the destruction of the temple; *i.e.*, from the Pharisee-sect to which Josephus belonged. It was a conclusion of orthodox Judaism. With true critical instinct, Spinoza says that the canon was the work of the Pharisees. The third collection was undoubtedly made under their influence.

The origin of the *threefold* division of the canon is not, as Oehler supposes,[1] a reflection of the different stages of religious development

---

[1] Article "Kanon" in Herzog's *Encyklopædie*, vol. vii., p. 253; and the same author's *Prolegomena zur Theologie des alt. Test.*, pp. 91, 92.

through which the nation passed, as if the foundation were the Law, the ulterior tendency in its objective aspect the Prophets, and its subjective aspect the Hagiographa. The books of Chronicles and others refute this arbitrary conception. The triplicity lies in the manner in which the books were collected. Men who belonged to different periods and possessed different degrees of culture worked successively in the formation of the canon; which arose out of the circumstances of the times, and the subjective ideas of those who made it.

The places of the separate books within the first division or *Torah*, were determined by the succession of the historical events narrated. The second division naturally begins with Moses's successor, Joshua. Judges, Samuel, and Kings follow according to the regular chronology. To the former prophets, as Joshua —Kings were called, the latter were attached,

Isaiah, Jeremiah, and Ezekiel; succeeded by the twelve minor prophets, arranged for the most part according to their times, though the length of individual prophecies and similarity of contents also influenced their position. The arrangement of books in the third division depended on their age, character, and authors. The Psalms were put first, because David was supposed to be the author of many, and on account of their intrinsic value in promoting the religious life of the people. After the Psalms came the three poetical works attributed to Solomon, with the book of Job among them,—Proverbs, Job, Canticles, Ecclesiastes. The book of Esther followed, since it was intended to further the observance of the Purim feast; with the late book of Daniel. The position of Daniel among the *c'tubim* arises solely from the fact of its posterior origin to the prophetic writings, not excepting the book of Jonah itself; and the attempt to account for its place in the third division on the ground of its predominant subjectivity is based on the unfounded assumption that the objective state of religion is represented in the second division and the subjective in the third. Had the book existed before 400 B.C., it would doubtless have stood in the second division. But the contents themselves demonstrate its date; contemporary history being wrapped in a prophetic form. Having some affinity to Esther as regards heathenism and Greek life, the book was put next to the latter. To Ezra and Nehemiah, which were adopted before the other part of the Chronicle-book and separated from it, were added the so-called Chronicles. Such was the original succession of the third division or *c'tubim;* but it did not remain unaltered. For the use of the synagogue the five Megiloth were put together; so that Ruth, which was originally appended to Judges, and the Lamentations affixed at first to Jeremiah's prophecies, were taken out of the second and put into the third canon. This caused a separation of Canticles and Ecclesiastes. The new arrangement was made for liturgical purposes.

CHAPTER III.

THE SAMARITAN AND ALEXANDRIAN CANONS.

THE Samaritan canon consists of the Pentateuch alone. This restricted collection is owing to the fact, that when the Samaritans separated from the Jews and began their worship on Gerizim, no more than the Mosaic writings had been invested by Ezra with canonical dignity. The hostile feeling between the rivals hindered the reception of books subsequently canonized. The idea of their having the oldest and most sacred part in its entirety satisfied their spiritual wants. Some have thought that the Sadducees, who already existed as a party before the Maccabean period, agreed with the Samaritans in rejecting all but the Pentateuch; yet this is doubtful. It is true that the Samaritans themselves say so;[1] and that some of the church fathers, Origen, Jerome, and others agree; but little reliance can be put on the statement. The latter, perhaps, confounded the Samaritans and Sadducees. It is also noteworthy that Christ in refuting the Sadducees appeals to the Pentateuch alone; yet the conclusion, that he did so because of their admitting no more than that portion does not follow.

The Alexandrian canon differed from the Palestinian. The Greek translation commonly called the Septuagint contains some later productions which the Palestinian Jews did not adopt, not only from their aversion to Greek literature generally, but also from the recent origin of the books, perhaps also their want of prophetic sanction. The closing line of the third part in the Alexandrian canon was more or less

[1] See Abulfatach's *Annal. Samar.*, p. 102, 9, &c.

fluctuating—capable of admitting recent writings appearing under the garb of old names and histories, or embracing religious subjects; while the Palestinian collection was pretty well determined, and all but finally settled. The judgment of the Alexandrians was freer than that of their brethren in the mother country. They had even separated in a measure from the latter, by erecting a temple at Leontopolis; and their enlargement of the canon was another step of divergence. Nor had they the criterion of language for the separation of canonical and uncanonical; both classes were before them in the same tongue. The enlarged canon was not formally sanctioned; it had not the approval of the Sanhedrim; yet it was to the Alexandrians what the Palestinian one was to the Palestinians. If Jews who were not well acquainted with Hebrew used the apocryphal and canonical books alike, it was a matter of feeling and custom; and if those who knew the old language better adhered to the canonical more closely, it was a matter of tradition and language. The former set little value on the prevalent consciousness of the race that the spirit of prophecy was extinct; their view of the Spirit's operation was larger. The latter clung to the past with all the more tenacity that the old life of the nation had degenerated.

The Alexandrian Jews opened their minds to Greek culture and philosophy, appropriating new ideas, and explaining their Scriptures in accordance with wider conceptions of the divine presence; though such adaptation turned aside the original sense. Consciously or unconsciously they were preparing Judaism in some degree to be the religion of humanity. But the Rabbins shut out those enlarging-influences, confining their religion within the narrow traditions of one people. The process by which they conserved the old belief helped to quench its spirit, so that it became an antique skeleton, powerless

beside the new civilisation which had followed
the wake of Alexander's conquests. Rabbinical
Judaism proved its incapacity for regenerating
the world ; having no affinity for the philosophy
of second causes, or for the exercise of reason
beneath the love of a Father who sees with equal
eye as God of all. Its isolation nourished a
sectarian tendency. Tradition, having no creative power like revelation, had taken the place
of it ; and it could not ward off the senility of
Judaism; for its creations are but feeble echoes
of prophetic utterances, weak imitations of poetic
inspiration or of fresh wisdom. They are of the
understanding rather than the reason. The tradition which Geiger describes as the life-giving
soul of Judaism—the daughter of revelation,
enjoying the same rights with her mother—a
spiritual power that continues ever to work—an
emanation from the divine Spirit—is not, indeed,
the thing which has stiffened Judaism into Rabbinism ; but neither is it tradition proper ; it is

reason working upon revelation, and moulding it into a new system. *Such tradition* serves but to show the inability of genuine Judaism to assimilate philosophic thought. *Rationalising* should not be styled the operation of tradition.

The truth of these remarks is evident from a comparison of two books, exemplifying Alexandrian and Palestinian Judaism respectively. The Wisdom of Solomon shows the enlarging effect of Greek philosophy. Overpassing Jewish particularism, it often approaches Christianity in doctrine and spirit, so that some[1] have even assumed a Christian origin for it. The Wisdom of Jesus son of Sirach has not the doctrine of immortality. Death is there an eternal sleep, and retribution takes place in this life. The Jewish theocracy is the centre of history; Israel the elect people; and all wisdom is embodied in the law. The writer is shut up within the old national ideas, and leans upon the writings in

Kirschbaum, Weisse, and Noack.

which they are expressed. Thus the Hagiographical canon of Judea, conservative as it is, and purer in a sense, presents a narrower type than the best specimens of the Alexandrian one. The genial breath of Aryan culture had not expanded its Semitism.

The identity of the Palestinian and Alexandrian canons must be abandoned, notwithstanding the contrary arguments of Eichhorn and Movers. It is said, indeed, that Philo neither mentions nor quotes the Greek additions; but neither does he quote several canonical books. According to Eichhorn, no fewer than eight of the latter are unnoticed by him.[1] Besides, he had peculiar views of inspiration, and quoted loosely from memory. Believing as he did in the inspiration of the Greek version as a whole, it is difficult to think that he made a distinction between the different parts of it. In one passage he refers to the sacred

[1] *Einleitung in das alte Testament*, vol. i. p. 133.

books of the Therapeutae, a fanatical sect of Jews in Egypt, as "*laws*, oracles *of prophets, hymns* and *other books* by which knowledge and piety are increased and perfected,"[1] but this presents little information as to the canon of the Egyptian Jews generally; for it is precarious argumentation to say with Herbst that they prove a twofold canon. Even if the Alexandrian and Palestinian canons be identical, we cannot be sure that *the other books* which the Therapeutae read as holy besides the law, *the prophets and hymns*, differed from the hagiographa, and so constituted another canon than the general Egyptian one. It is quite possible that *the hymns* mean the Psalms; and *the other books*, the rest of the hagiographa. The argument for the identity of the two canons deduced from 4 Esdras xiv. 44, &c., as if the twenty-four open books were distinguished from the other writings dictated to

[1] *De vita contemplativa*, Opp. Tom. ii., p. 475, ed. Mangey.

Ezra, is of no force, because verisimilitude required that an Egyptian Jew himself must make Ezra conform to the old Palestinian canon. It is also alleged that the grandson of Jesus Sirach, who translated his grandfather's work during his abode in Egypt, knew no difference between the Hebrew and Greek canon, though he speaks of the Greek version; but he speaks as a Palestinian, without having occasion to allude to the difference between the canonical books of the Palestinian and Egyptian Jews. The latter may have reckoned the apocryphal writings in the third division; and therefore the translator of Jesus Sirach could recognise them in the ordinary classification. The mention of *three* classes is not opposed to their presence in the third. The general use of an enlarged canon in Egypt cannot be denied, though it was somewhat loose, not regarded as a completed collection, and without express rabbinical sanction. If they did not *formally* recognise a canon of their own, as De Wette says of them, they had and used one larger than the Palestinian, without troubling themselves about a *formal* sanction for it by a body of Rabbis at Jerusalem or elsewhere. Their canon was not identical with that of the Palestinians, and all the argumentation founded upon Philo's non-quotation of the apocryphal books fails to prove the contrary. The very way in which apocryphal are inserted among canonical books in the Alexandrian canon, shows the equal rank assigned to both. Esdras first and second succeed the Chronicles; Tobit and Judith are between Nehemiah and Esther; the Wisdom of Solomon and Sirach follow Canticles; Baruch succeeds Jeremiah; Daniel is followed by Susanna and other productions of the same class; and the whole closes with the three books of Maccabees. Such is the order in the Vatican MS.

The threefold division of the canon, indicating three stages in its formation, has continued. Josephus, indeed, gives another, based on the nature of the separate books, not on MSS. We learn nothing from him of its history, which is somewhat remarkable, considering that he did not live two centuries after the last work had been added. The account of the canon's final arrangement was evidently unknown to him.

CHAPTER IV.

NUMBER AND ORDER OF THE SEPARATE BOOKS.

THE number of the books was variously estimated. Josephus gives twenty-two, which was the usual number among Christian writers in the second, third, and fourth centuries, having been derived perhaps from the letters of the Hebrew alphabet. Origen, Jerome, and others have it. It continued longest among the teachers of the Greek Church, and is even in Nicephorus's stichometry.[1] The enumeration in question has Ruth with Judges, and Lamentations with Jeremiah. In Epiphanius[2] the number twenty-seven is found, made by taking the alphabet

[1] See Credner's *Zur Geschichte des Kanons*, p. 124.

[2] *De mens. et pond.*, chapters 22, 23, vol. ii. p. 180, ed. Petav.

enlarged with the five final letters, and dividing Samuel, Kings, and Chronicles into two books each. This is probably an ingenious combination belonging to the father himself. The Talmud has twenty-four,[1] a number which did not originate in the Greek alphabet, else the Palestinian Jews would not have adopted it. The synagogue did not fix it officially. After the Pentateuch and the former prophets, which are in the usual order, it gives Jeremiah as the first of the later, succeeded by Ezekiel and Isaiah with the twelve minor prophets. The Talmud knows no other reason for such an order than that it was made according to the contents of the prophetic books, not according to the times of the writers. This solution is unsatisfactory. It is more probable that chronology had to do with the arrangement.[2] After the anonymous collection or second part of Isaiah had been joined to the

---

[1] *Baba Bathra*, fol. 14, 2.
[2] See *Fürst, Der Kanon u. s. w.* p. 14, &c.

first or authentic prophecies, the lateness of these oracles brought Isaiah into the third place among the greater prophets. The Talmudic order of the Hagiographa is Ruth, Psalms, Job, Proverbs, Ecclesiastes, Canticles, Lamentations, Daniel, Esther, Ezra, Chronicles. Here Ruth precedes the Psalter, coming as near the former prophets as possible; for it properly belongs to them, the contents associating it with the Judges' time. The Talmudic order is that usually adopted in German MSS. What is the true estimate of it? Is it a proper Talmudic regulation? Perhaps not, else the Hebrew MSS. of the French and Spanish Jews would not so readily have departed from it. Bloch supposes that Baba Bathra, which gives the arrangement of the books, is one of the apocryphal Boraithas that proceeded from an individual teacher and had no binding authority.[1]

[1] *Studien zur Geschichte der alttestamentliche Literatur, u. s. w.*, p. 18, etc.

The Masoretic arrangement differs from the Talmudic in putting Isaiah before Jeremiah and Ezekiel. The Hagiographa are, Psalms, Proverbs, Job, Canticles, Ruth, Lamentations, Ecclesiastes, Esther, Daniel, Ezra (with Nehemiah), Chronicles.[1] This is usually adopted in Spanish MSS. But MSS. often differ arbitrarily, because transcribers did not consider themselves bound to any one arrangement.[2] According to some, a very old testimony to the commencing and concluding books of the third division is given by the New Testament (Luke xxiv. 44; Matthew xxiii. 35), agreeably to which the Psalms were first and the Chronicles last; but this is inconclusive.

The Alexandrian translators, as we have seen already, placed the books differently from

[1] Hody, *De Bibliorum textibus originalibus*, p. 644.

[2] Hody gives lists of the order in which the books stand in some early printed editions and in a few MSS., p. 645.

the Palestinian Jews. In their version Daniel comes after Ezekiel, so that it is put beside the greater prophets. Was this done by Jews or Christians? Perhaps by the latter, who put it between the greater and lesser prophets, or in other words, out of the third into the second division, because of dogmatic grounds, and so effaced a trace of the correct chronology. Little importance, however, can be attached to the order of the books in the Septuagint; because the work was done at different times by different persons. But whatever may have been the arrangement of the parts when the whole was complete, we know that it was disturbed by Protestants separating the apocryphal writings and putting them all together.

CHAPTER V.

USE OF THE OLD TESTAMENT BY THE FIRST CHRISTIAN WRITERS, AND BY THE FATHERS TILL THE TIME OF ORIGEN.

THE writings of the New Testament show the authors' acquaintance with the apocryphal books. They have expressions and ideas derived from them. Stier collected one hundred and two passages which bear some resemblance to others in the Apocrypha;[1] but they needed sifting, and were cut down to a much smaller number by Bleek. They are James i. 19, from Sirach v. 11 and iv. 29; 1 Peter i. 6, 7, from Wisdom iii. 3-7; Hebrews xi. 34, 35, from 2 Maccabees vi. 18—vii. 42; Hebrews i. 3, from Wisdom vii. 26, &c.; Romans i. 20-32, from

[1] *Die Apokryphen, u. s. w.*, p. 14, &c.

Wisdom xiii.-xv.; Romans ix. 21, from Wisdom xv. 7; Eph. vi. 13-17, from Wisdom v. 18-20; 1 Cor. ii. 10, &c., from Judith viii. 14. Others are less probable.[1] When Bishop Cosin says, that "in all the New Testament we find not any one passage of the apocryphal books to have been alleged either by Christ or His apostles for the confirmation of their doctrine,"[2] the argument, though based on fact, is scarcely conclusive; else Esther, Canticles, Ecclesiastes, and other works might be equally discredited. Yet it is probable that the New Testament writers, though quoting the Septuagint much more than the original, were disinclined to the additional parts of the Alexandrian canon. They were Palestinian themselves, or had in view Judaisers of a narrow creed. Prudential motives, no less than a predisposition in favour of the old national canon, may have hindered

---

[1] *Studien und Kritiken* for 1853, p. 267, &c.
[2] *A Scholastical History of the Canon*, p. 22.

them from expressly citing any apocryphal production. The apostle Paul and probably the other writers of the New Testament, believed in the literal inspiration of the Biblical books, for he uses an argument in the Galatian epistle which turns upon the singular or plural of a noun.[1] And as the inspiration of the Septuagint translation was commonly held by the Christians of the early centuries, it may be that the apostles and evangelists made no distinction between its parts. Jude quotes Enoch, an apocryphal work not in the Alexandrian canon; so that he at

---

[1] See Rothe, *Zur Dogmatik, Studien u. Kritiken* for 1860, p. 67, &c. The apostle's argument rests on the occurrence of the singular (*seed*, σπέρμα) in Genesis xvii. 8 (LXX.), not the plural (*seeds*, σπέρματα); though the plural of the corresponding Hebrew word could not have been used, because it has a different signification. Grammatical inaccuracy is made the basis of a certain theological interpretation. Those who wish to see a specimen of laboured ingenuity unsuccessfully applied to the justification of St Paul's argument in this passage, may consult Tholuck's *Das alte Testament in neuem Testament*, p. 63, etc. Vierte Auflage. (Epist. to the Galatians iii. 16.)

least had no rigid notions about the difference of canonical and uncanonical writings. Still we know that the compass of the Old Testament canon was somewhat unsettled to the Christians of the first century, as it was to the Hellenist Jews themselves. It is true that the Law, the Prophets, and the Psalms were universally recognized as authoritative; but the extent of the third division was indefinite, so that the non-citation of the three books respecting which there was a difference of opinion among the Jews may not have been accidental. Inasmuch, however, as the Greek-speaking Jews received more books than their Palestinian brethren, the apostles and their immediate successors were not wholly disinclined to the use of the apocryphal productions. The undefined boundary of the canon facilitated also the recognition of all primitive records of the new Revelation.

The early fathers, who wrote in Greek, used the

Greek Bible, as almost all of them were ignorant of Hebrew. Thus restricted, they naturally considered its parts alike, citing apocryphal and canonical in the same way. Accordingly, Irenæus[1] quotes Baruch under the name of "Jeremiah the prophet;"[2] and the additions to Daniel as "Daniel the prophet."[3] Clement of Alexandria[4] uses the apocryphal books like the canonical ones, for explanation and proof indiscriminately. He is fond of referring to Baruch, which he cites upwards of twenty-four times in the second book of his *Pædagogus*, and in a manner to show that he esteemed it as highly as many other parts of the Old Testament. A passage from Baruch is introduced by the phrase,[5] "the divine Scripture says;" and another from Tobit

---

[1] † 202 A.D.

[2] *Advers. Hares.*, v. 35, referring to Baruch iv. 36; and v. p. 335, ed. Massuet.

[3] *Ibid.* iv., 26, referring to Daniel xiii. 20 in the Septuagint.

[4] † 220 A.D.   [5] *Pædagog.* ii. 3.

by [1] "Scripture has briefly signified this, saying." Assuming that Wisdom was written by Solomon, he uses it as canonical and inspired, designating it *divine*.[2] Judith he cites with other books of the Old Testament[3]; and the Song of the three children in the furnace is used as Scripture.[4] Ecclesiasticus also is so treated.[5] Dionysius of Alexandria[6] cites Ecclesiasticus (xvi. 26), introducing the passage with "hear divine oracles."[7] The same book is elsewhere cited, chapters xliii. 29, 30[8] and i. 8. 9.[9] So is Wisdom, vii. 15[10] and 25.[11] Baruch (iii. 12-15) is also quoted.[12] The fathers who wrote in Latin used some of the old Latin versions of which Augustine speaks; one of them, and that the

---

[1] *Stromata*, ii. 23.   [2] *Stromata*, iv. 16.   [3] *Ibid*, ii. 7.
[4] *Ex Script. prophet. eclogae*, c. 1.
[5] *Stromateis*, ii. 15.   [6] † 264 A.D.
[7] *De Natura; Routh's Reliquiae Sacrae*, vol. iv. p. 356.
[8] *Fragment. Nicet.*, in *Reliq. Sacrae*, vol. ii. p. 404.
[9] *Ibid.*, p. 407.   [10] *Ibid.*, p. 406.
[11] *Epistola ad. Dionys. Roman*, in *Reliq. Sacr.*, vol. iii. p. 195.
[12] *Reliq. Sacr.*, vol. ii. p. 408.

oldest, probably dating soon after the middle of the second century, being known to us as the *Itala*. As this was made from the Septuagint, it had the usual apocryphal books. Jerome's critical revision or new version did not supplant the old Latin till some time after his death. Tertullian[1] quotes the Wisdom of Solomon expressly as Solomon's;[2] and introduces Sirach by "as it is written."[3] He cites Baruch as Jeremiah.[4] He also believes in the authenticity of the book of Enoch, and defends it as *Scripture* at some length.[5] Cyprian often cites the Greek additions to the Palestinian canon. He introduces Tobit with the words "as it is written,"[6] or "divine Scripture teaches, saying;"[7] and Wisdom with, "the Holy Spirit shows by Solomon."[8] Ecclesiasticus is intro-

---

[1] † 220 A.D.   [2] *Advers. Valentinianos*, ch. 2.
[3] *De Exhortatione Castitatis*, ch. 2.
[4] *Contra Gnosticos*, ch. 8.   [5] *De Habitu Muliebri*, ch. 3.
[6] *Epist.* 55, p. 110, ed. Fell.   [7] *De Orat. Domin.*, p. 153.
[8] *De Exhortat. Martyrii*, ch. 12, p. 182.

duced with, "it is written;"[1] and Baruch with, "the Holy Spirit teaches by Jeremiah."[2] 1 and 2 Maccabees are used as Scripture;[3] as are the additions to Daniel.[4] The African fathers follow the Alexandrian canon without scruple. Hippolytus of Rome (about A.D. 220), who wrote in Greek, quotes Baruch as Scripture;[5] and interprets the additions to Daniel, such as Susanna, as Scripture likewise.

Melito of Sardis[7] made it his special business to inquire among the Palestinian Jews about the number and names of their canonical books; and the result was the following list:—the five books of Moses, Joshua, Judges, Ruth, four books of Kings, two of Chronicles, the Psalms of David, the Proverbs of Solomon, Ecclesiastes, the Song of Songs, Job, Isaiah, Jeremiah, the twelve in one book,

[1] *De Mortal*, p. 161.
[2] *De Orat. Domin.*, p. 141.
[3] *Testim.* iii. 4, p. 62.
[4] *De Lapsis*, p. 133, &c.
[5] *Adv. Noet.* v.
[6] See Migne's edition, p. 689, &c.
[7] † After 171.

Daniel, Ezekiel, Ezra.[1] Here Ezra includes Nehemiah; and Esther is absent, because the Jews whom he consulted did not consider it canonical.

Origen's[2] list does not differ much from the Palestinian one. After the Pentateuch, Joshua, Judges, Ruth, Kings first and second, Samuel, Chronicles, come Ezra first and second, Psalms, Proverbs, Ecclesiastes, Canticles, Isaiah, Jeremiah with Lamentations and the epistle, Daniel, Ezekiel, Job, Esther. Besides these there are the Maccabees, which are inscribed *Sarbeth Sarbane el*.[3] The twelve prophets are omitted in the Greek; but the mistake is rectified in Rufinus's Latin version, where they follow Canticles, as in Hilary and Cyril of Jerusalem. It is remarkable that Baruch is given, and why? Because Origen took it from the MSS. of the Septuagint he had before him, in which the

---
[1] *Ap*. Euseb. H. E., lib. iv. ch. 26.   [2] † 254 A.D.
[3] *Ap*. Euseb. H. E., lib. vi. ch. 25.

epistle is attributed to Jeremiah. But the catalogue had no influence upon his practice. He followed the prevailing view of the extended canon. Sirach is introduced by "for this also *is written*";[1] the book of Wisdom is cited as *a divine word*;[2] the writer is called *a prophet*;[3] *Christ* is represented as speaking in it *through Solomon*;[4] and Wisdom vii. 17 is adduced as *the words of Christ Himself*.[5] Tobit is cited as *Scripture*.[6] His view of the additions to the books of Daniel and Esther, as well as his opinion about Tobit, are sufficiently expressed in the epistle to Africanus, so that scattered quotations from these parts of Scripture can be properly estimated. Of the history of Susanna he ventures to say that the Jews

---

[1] *Comment. in Joann.*, tom. xxxii. ch. 14, ed. Huet. p. 409.
[2] *Contra Cels.* iii. 72 ; vol. i. p. 494, ed. Delarue.
[3] *In Exodus*, Hom. vi. 1 ; Levit. Hom. v. 2.
[4] *In Levit.*, Hom. xii. 4.
[5] *In Lukam*, Hom. 21.
[6] *De Oratione*, ii. p. 215.

withdrew it on purpose from the people.¹ He seems to argue in favour of books used and read in the churches, though they may be put out of the canon by the Jews. As divine Providence had preserved the sacred Scriptures, no alteration should be made in the ecclesiastical tradition respecting books sanctioned by the churches though they be external to the Hebrew canon.

Most of the writings of Methodius Bishop of Tyre[2] are lost, so that we know little of his opinions respecting the books of Scripture. But it is certain that he employed the Apocrypha like the other writings of the Old Testament. Thus Sirach (xviii. 30 and xix. 2) is quoted in the same way as the Proverbs.[3] Wisdom (iv. 1-3) is cited,[4] and Baruch (iii. 14).[5]

---

[1] *Opp.* ed. Delarue, vol. i. p. 12.

[2] † 311.

[3] *Convivium decem virginum*, in Combefis's Auctarium bibliothecæ Græcorum patrum, p. 69.

[4] *Ibid.*, p. 69.   [5] *Ibid.*, p. 109.

CHAPTER VI.

THE NEW TESTAMENT CANON IN THE FIRST THREE CENTURIES.

THE first Christians relied on the Old Testament as their chief religious book. To them it was of divine origin and authority. The New Testament writings came into gradual use, by the side of the older Jewish documents, according to the times in which they appeared and the names of their reputed authors. The Epistles of Paul were the earliest written; after which came the Apocalypse, the Epistle to the Hebrews, and other documents, all in the first century. After the first gospel had undergone a process of translation, re-writing, and interpolation, from the Aramaic basis, *the discourses*,[1] of which

[1] τὰ λόγια. *Ap.* Euseb. H. .E. iii. 39.

Papias of Hierapolis speaks, until the traces of another original than the Greek were all but effaced; it appeared in its present form early in the second century. Soon after that of Luke was composed, whose prevailing Pauline tendency was not allowed to suppress various features of a Jewish Essene type. The second gospel, which bears evidences of its derivation from the other synoptists, was followed by the fourth. The last document was the so-called second Epistle of Peter. It is manifest that tradition assumed various forms after the death of Jesus; that legend and myth speedily surrounded His sacred person; that the unknown writers were influenced by the peculiar circumstances in which they stood with respect to Jewish and Gentile Christianity; and that their uncritical age dealt considerably in the marvellous. That the life of the great Founder should be overlaid with extraneous materials, is special matter for regret. However conscientious and truth-loving they may have been, the reporters were unequal to their work. It is also remarkable that so many of them should be unknown; productions being attached to names of repute to give them greater currency.

When Marcion came from Pontus to Rome (144 A.D.,) he brought with him a Scripture-collection consisting of ten Pauline epistles. With true critical instinct he did not include those addressed to Timothy and Titus, as also the epistle to the Hebrews. The gospel of Marcion was Luke's in an altered state. From this and other facts we conclude that external parties were the first who carried out the idea of collecting Christian writings, and of putting them either beside or over against the sacred books of the Old Testament, in support of their systems. As to Basilides (125 A.D.), his supposed quotations from the New Testament in Hippolytus are too precarious to be trusted.[1]

[1] Davidson's *Introduction to the Study of the N. Testam.*, vol. x. p. 388.

Testimonies to the "acknowledged" books of the New Testament as Scripture have been transferred from his followers to himself; so that his early witness to the canon breaks down. It is inferred from statements in Origen and Jerome that he had a gospel of his own somewhat like St Luke's, but extra-canonical. His son Isidore and succeeding disciples used Matthew's gospel. Jerome says that Marcion and Basilides denied the Pauline authorship of the epistle to the Hebrews and the pastoral ones.[1] It is also doubtful whether Valentinus's (140-166 A.D.) alleged citations from the New Testament can be relied upon. The passages of this kind ascribed to him by the fathers belong in a great measure to his disciples. The fragment of a letter preserved by Clement of Alexandria in the second book of the Stromata, has been thought to contain references to the gospels of Matthew

[1] *Explanatio in Epist. ad Titum*, vol. iv. p. 407, ed. Benedict.

and Luke; but the fact is doubtful. Nor has Henrici proved that Valentinus used John's gospel.[1] But his followers, including Ptolemy (180 A.D.) and Heracleon (185-200 A.D.), quote the Gospels and other portions of the New Testament.[2] From Hippolytus's account of the Ophites, Peratæ, and Sethians, we infer that the Christian writings were much employed by them. They rarely cite an apocryphal work. More than one hundred and sixty citations from the New Testament have been gathered out of their writings.[3] We may admit that these Ophites and Peratæ were of early origin, the former being the oldest known of the Gnostic parties; but there is no proof that the acquaintance with the New Testament

[1] *Die Valentinianische Gnosis und die heilige Schrift*, p. 75.

[2] A good deal of manipulation has been needlessly employed for the purpose of placing these heretics as early as possible; but nothing definite can be extracted from Irenæus's notices of them. Hippolytus's use of the present tense, in speaking of them, renders it probable that they were nearly his contemporaries.

[3] See the Indexes to Duncker and Schneidewin's edition.

which Hippolytus attributes to them belongs to the first rather than the second half of the second century. The early existence of the sect does not show an early citation of the Christian books by it, especially of John's gospel; unless its primary were its last stage. Later and earlier Ophites are not distinguished in the *Philosophumena*. Hence there is a presumption that the author had the former in view, which is favoured by no mention of them occurring in the "Adversus omnes Hæreses" usually appended to Tertullian's *Præscriptiones Hæreticorum*, and by Irenæus's derivation of their heresy from that of Valentinus. The latter father does not even speak of the Peratæ. Clement of Alexandria is the first who alludes to them. The early heretics were desirous of confirming their peculiar opinions by the writings current among Catholic Christians, so that the formation of a canon by them began soon after the commencement of the second century, and continued till the end of it; contemporaneously with the development of a Catholic Church and its necessary adjunct a Catholic canon.

No New Testament canon, except a partial and unauthoritative one, existed till the latter half of the second century, that is, till the idea of a Catholic church began to be entertained. The living power of Christianity in its early stages had no need of books for its nurture. But in the development of a church organization the internal rule of consciousness was changed into an external one of faith. The Ebionites or Jewish Christians had their favourite Gospels and Acts. The gospel of Matthew was highly prized by them, existing as it did in various recensions, of which the gospel according to the Hebrews was one. Other documents, such as the Revelation of John; and the preaching of Peter, a Jewish-Christian history subsequently re-written and employed in the Clementine Recognitions and Homilies, were also in esteem. Even so late as 175-180 A.D., Hegesippus, a Jewish Christian, does not seem to have had a canon consisting of the four gospels and Paul's Epistles, but appeals to "the law and the prophets and *the Lord*," so that his leading principle was, the identity of Jesus's words with the Old Testament; agreeably to the tenets of the party he belonged to. The source whence he drew the words of Jesus was probably the Gospel according to the Hebrews, a document which we know he used, on the authority of Eusebius. He does not refer to Paul except by implication in a passage given in Photius from Stephen Gobar,[1] where he says that such as used the words "Eye hath not seen, nor ear heard," &c., falsified the Divine Scriptures and the Lord's words, "Blessed are your eyes for they see,"

[1] *Bibliotheca*, cod. 232.

&c. As Paul quoted the condemned language, he is blamed.[1] Though he knew Paul's epistles, he does not look upon them as *authoritative*. He betrays no acquaintance with the fourth gospel; for the question, "What is the door to Jesus?" does not presuppose the knowledge of John x. 2, 7, 9. Nösgen has failed to prove Hegesippus's Jewish descent; and Holtzmann's mediating view of him is incorrect.[2]

---

[1] It is an unfounded assumption that Paul cited the passage by "mere accident"; on the contrary, he gives it as canonical, with "as it is written" (1 Corinth. ii. 9). It may be that the Gnostics are referred to as using the objectionable passage; but it is special pleading *to limit* it to them, when Paul has expressly used the same, deriving it either from Isaiah lxiv. 4, or some unknown document; just as it is special pleading to identify ὁ κύριος standing beside νόμος καὶ προφῆται, with *the New Testament*. The word excludes Paul's Epistles from the canon; nor is there any evidence to the contrary, as has been alleged, in the two Syriac epistles attributed to Clement, which Wetstein published. Comp. *Eusebius's H. E.* iv. 22, *Photius's Bibliotheca*, 232. Apologists have laboured to prove Hegesippus an orthodox Catholic Christian, like Irenaeus; but in vain. He was a Jewish Christian of moderate type, holding intercourse with Pauline Christians at the time when the Catholic Church was being formed.

[2] See *Hilgenfeld's Zeitschrift* for 1875-1878.

The Clementine Homilies (161-180 A.-D. used the four canonical gospels even the fourth (which is somewhat singular in a writer who denies the deity of Christ), and assigned it to the apostle John. The gospel according to the Egyptians was also employed. Paul's epistles were rejected of course, as well as the Acts; since the apostle of the Gentiles was pointed at in Simon Magus, whom Peter refutes. It is, therefore, obvious that a collection of the New Testament writings could make little progress among the Ebionites of the second century. Their reverence for the law and the prophets hindered another canon. Among the Gentile Christians the formation of a canon took place more rapidly, though Judaic influences retarded it even there. After Paul's epistles were interchanged between churches a few of them would soon be put together. A collection of this kind is implied in 2 Peter iii. 16. The pastoral epistles, which show their dependence on the authentic Pauline ones, with those of Peter, presuppose a similar collection; which, along with the Synoptists, existed before the fourth gospel. The Apocalypse and the epistle to the Hebrews were obnoxious to the Pauline churches, as Paul's letters were to the Jewish-Christian ones. Hence the former were outside the Pauline collections.

The apostolic fathers quote from the Old Testament, which was sacred and inspired to them. They have scarcely any express citations from the New Testament. *Allusions* occur, especially to the epistles.

The first Epistle of Clement to the Corinthians (about 120 A.D.), implies acquaintance with several of the epistles, with those to the Corinthians, Romans, Hebrews, and perhaps others. Two passages have also been adduced as derived from the gospels of Matthew and Luke, viz., in chapters xiii. 2 and xlvi. 8; but probably some other source supplied them, such as oral tradition. It has also been argued that the quotation in the fifteenth chapter, "The Scripture says somewhere, This people honoureth me with their lips, but their heart is far from me," comes from Mark vii. 6 in which it varies from the Hebrew of Isaiah xxix. 13, as well as the Septuagint version. Clement therefore, so it is said, quotes the Old Testament through the medium of the gospels (Matthew xv. 8, Mark vii. 6). But the argument is inconclusive because the words agree closely enough with the Septuagint to render the supposition very probable that they are a memoriter citation from it. As they stand, they coincide exactly neither with Mark nor the Septuagint.[1] Thus we dissent from the opinion of Gebhardt and Harnack. Wherever "Scripture" is cited, or the expres-

[1] There is ἄπεστιν instead of the Septuagint's and Mark's (Tischend.) ἀπέχει.

sion "it is written" occurs, the Old Testament is meant.

Hermas (about 140 A.D.) seems to have used the epistle to the Ephesians and perhaps that to the Hebrews, as well as the epistle of James; but there is great uncertainty about the matter, for there is no *express* or certain quotation from any part of the New Testament. The writer often alludes to words of Jesus, found in Matthew's gospel, so that he may have been acquainted with it. Keim[1] and others have discovered references to the fourth gospel; but they are invalid. There is no allusion to the Acts in vis. iv. 2, 4. The only *Scripture* cited is the apocryphal book *Eldat and Modat*, now lost.[2] The writer seems to have known several Jewish Apocalypses.[3]

[1] *Geschichte Jesu von Nazara*, vol. I, p. 144.

[2] See Vision ii. 3, 4, with the prolegomena of De Gebhardt and Harnack, p. lxxiii.

[3] See Holtzmann in Hilgenfeld's *Zeitschrift* for 1875, p. 40, &c.

Barnabas (about 119 A.D.) has but one quotation from the New Testament, if, indeed, it be such. Apparently, Matthew xx. 16 or xxii. 14 is introduced by "as it is written," showing that the gospel was considered *Scripture*.[1] This is the earliest trace of canonical authority being transferred from the Old Testament to Christian writings. But the citation is not certain. The original may be 4 Esdras viii. 3; and even if the writer took the words from Matthew's gospel, it is possible that he used "it is written" with reference to their prototype in the Old Testament. Of such interchanges examples occur in writers of the second century; and it is the more probable that this is one, from the fact that 4 Esdras is elsewhere considered a prophet and referred to in the same way as Ezekiel.[2] Barnabas's citation of a gospel as canonical is wholly improbable, since

[1] Epist. ch. iv.
[2] Chapter xii. pp. 30, 31, ed. 2, Hilgenfeld.

even Justin, thirty years after, never quotes the New Testament writings as *Scripture*. The thing would be anomalous and opposed to the history of the first half of the second century. When these post-apostolic productions appeared, the New Testament writings did not stand on the same level with the Old, and were not yet esteemed *sacred* and *inspired* like the Jewish Scriptures. The Holy Spirit was thought to dwell in all Christians, without being confined to a few writers; and his influence was the common heritage of believers. There are evidences of Barnabas's acquaintance with the Epistles to the Romans and Corinthians; nor is it improbable that he knew the canonical gospel of Matthew, though one passage *appears* to contradict Matthew xxviii. 10, &c., without necessarily implying ignorance of what lies in it, viz., that the ascension of Jesus took place on the day of his resurrection.[1] Strangely enough,

[1] See Chapter xv. end, with Hilgenfeld's note, *Barnabae epistula ed. altera*, pp. 118, 119.

Keim thinks that the writer had John's gospel before him; but this opinion is refuted by the end of Barnabas's fifth chapter.[1] Holtzmann has ably disposed of the considerations adduced by Keim.[2] Barnabas quotes the book of Enoch as *Scripture;*[3] and an apocryphal prophecy is introduced with, "another prophet says."[4]

As far as we can judge from Eusebius's account of Papias[5] (about 150 A.D.), that writer knew nothing of a New Testament canon. He speaks

---

[1] *Epis.* p. 13 ed. Hilgenfeld.

[2] *Zeitschrift für wissenschaftliche Theologie*, 1871, p. 336, etc.

[3] Chapters xvi. and iv. In the former the reference is to Enoch lxxxix. 56, 66, 67, but the latter is not in the present book of Enoch, though Hilgenfeld thinks he has discovered it in lxxxix. 61-64 and xc. 17. (*Dillmann's Das Buch Henoch*, pp. 61, 63). Was another apocryphal Jewish book current in the time of Barnabas, under the name of Enoch; or did he confound one document with another, misled by the Greek translation of an apocalyptic work which had fallen into discredit? See Hilgenfeld's *Barnabae Epistula*, ed. 2 pp. 77, 78.

[4] Chapter xi.

[5] *Hist. Eccles.* iii. 39.

of Matthew and Mark; but it is most probable that he had documents which either formed the basis of our present Matthew and Mark, or were taken into them and written over.[1] According to Andreas of Cæsarea he was acquainted with the Apocalypse of John; while Eusebius testifies to his knowledge of 1 Peter and 1 John. But he had no conception of canonical authority attaching to any part of the New Testament. His language implies

[1] A small body of literature originating in the fragment of Papias preserved by Eusebius (Hist. Eccles. iii., 39, 1-4) has appeared; though it is difficult to obtain satisfactory conclusions. Not only have Weiffenbach and Leimbach written treatises on the subject, but other scholars have entered into it more or less fully,—Zahn, Steitz, Riggenbach, Hilgenfeld, Lipsius, Keim, Martens, Loman, Holtzmann, Hausrath, Tietz, and Lightfoot. The fragment is not of great weight in settling the authenticity of the four gospels. Indirectly indeed it throws some light on the connection of two evangelists with written memoirs of the life of Jesus; but it rather suggests than solves various matters of importance. It is tolerably clear that the gospels, if such they may be called, of which he speaks as written by Matthew and Mark, were not identical with the works now existing under the names of these evangelists; and that no safe conclusion can be drawn from Papias's silence about John's and Luke's as not

the opposite, in that he prefers unwritten tradition to the gospel he speaks of. He neither felt the want nor knew the existence of *inspired* gospels.

We need not notice the three short Syriac epistles attributed to Ignatius, as we do not believe them to be his, but of later origin. Traces of later ideas about the canonicity of the New Testament appear in the shorter Greek recension of the Ignatian epistles (about 175

---

then in existence. Neither the present gospels nor any other had been converted into *Scripture;* since he regarded oral traditions as more credible than written memoirs. Those who hold that the presbyter John was none other than the apostle, Eusebius having misunderstood the fragment and made a different John from the apostle, as well as the critics who deduce from the fragment the fact that John suffered martyrdom in Palestine, have not established these conclusions. Papias refers to the material he got for explaining the λογία, rather than the source whence they were drawn. But whether he learnt directly from the elders, or indirectly as the preposition (παρὰ) would seem to indicate, and whether the sentence beginning with "What Andrew," &c., (τί 'Ανδρέας κ. τ. λ.) stands in apposition to the "words of the elders," (τοὺς τῶν πρεσβυτέρων λόγους) or not, are things uncertain.

A.D.) There *the Gospel* and *the Apostles* are recognized as the constituents of the book.[1] The writer also used the Gospel according to the Hebrews, for there is a quotation from it in the epistle to the Smyrnians.[2] The second part of the collection seems to have wanted the epistle to the Ephesians.[3] The two leading parties, long antagonistic, had now become united; the apostles Peter and Paul being mentioned together.[4] In the Testaments of the twelve patriarchs (about 170 A.D.), Paul's life is said to be described in "holy books," *i.e.*, his own epistles and the Acts.[5]

Justin Martyr (150 A.D.) knew the first and third of the synoptic gospels. His use of Mark's does not appear. His knowledge of

---

[1] *Epist. ad Philadelph.*, ch. 5. See Hefele's note on the passage. The other well-known passage in chapter viii. is too uncertain in reading and meaning to be adduced here.

[2] Chapter iii.   [3] To the Ephesians, chapter xii.

[4] *Epist. ad Romanos*, iv.

[5] *Testam. Benj.* 11, p. 201, ed. Sinker.

the fourth is denied by many, and zealously defended by others. Thoma finds proofs that Justin knew it well, and used it freely as a text-book of gnosis, without recognizing it as the historical work of an apostle; an hypothesis encumbered with difficulties.[1] Whatever be said about Justin's acquaintance with this gospel; its existence before 140 A.D. is incapable either of decisive or probable proof; and this father's Logos-doctrine is less developed than the Johannine, because it is encumbered with the notion of miraculous birth by a virgin. The Johannine authorship has receded before the tide of modern criticism; and though this tide is arbitrary at times, it is here irresistible. Apologists should abstain from strong assertions on a point so difficult, as that each "gospel is distinctly recognized by him ;" for the noted passage in the dialogue

[1] *Zeitschrift für wissenschaftliche Theologie*, 1875, p. 490, et seq.

with Trypho does not support them.[1] It is pretty certain that he employed an extra-canonical gospel, the so-called gospel of the Hebrews. This Petrine document may be referred to in a passage which is unfortunately capable of a double interpretation.[2] He had also the older Acts of Pilate. Paul's epistles are never mentioned, though he doubtless knew them. Having little sympathy with Paulinism he attached his belief much more to the primitive apostles. The Apocalypse, 1 Peter, and 1 John he esteemed highly; the epistle to the Hebrews and the Acts he treated in the same

---

[1] Ἐν τοῖς ἀπομνημονεύμασι, ἅ φημι ὑπὸ τῶν ἀποστόλων αὐτοῦ καὶ τῶν ἐκείνοις παρακολουθησάντων συντετάχθαι. Sec. 103. Here "the apostles" are not necessarily Matthew and John. Apocryphal gospels then current bore the name of apostles or their attendants,—of Peter, James, Nicodemus, Matthias, &c.

[2] Καὶ τὸ εἰπεῖν μετωνομακέναι αὐτὸν Πέτρον καὶ γεγράφθαι ἐν τοῖς ἀπομνημονεύμασι αὐτοῦ γεγενημένον, καὶ τοῦτο, μετὰ τοῦ καὶ, κ.τ.λ. Dial. cum Tryph., 106. Here the pronoun αὐτοῦ probably refers to Peter. And the expression "his memoirs" can hardly mean Mark's gospel, since Jerome is the first that calls it such.

way as the Pauline writings. Justin's canon, as far as divine authority and inspiration are concerned, was the Old Testament. He was merely on the threshold of a divine canon made up of primitive Christian writings, and attributed no exclusive sanctity to those he used because they were not to him the only source of doctrine. Even of the Apocalypse he says, "A man among us named John, &c., wrote it."[1] In his time none of the gospels had been canonized, not even the synoptists, if, indeed, he knew them all. Oral tradition was the chief fountain of Christian knowledge, as it had been for a century. In his opinion this tradition was embodied in writing; but the documents in which he looked for all that related to Christ were not the gospels alone. He used others freely, not looking upon any as *inspired;* for that idea could arise only when a selection

[1] *Dialogus*, part ii., p. 315, ed. Thirlby. Comp. on Justin, Tjeenk-Willink's *Justinus Martyr in zijne Verhouding tot Paulus.*

was made among the current documents. He regarded them all as having been written down from memory, and judged them by criteria of evidence conformable to the Old Testament Scriptures. Though lessons out of Gospels (some of our present ones and others), as also out of the prophets, were read in assemblies on the first day of the week,[1] the act of converting the Christian writings into *Scripture* was posterior; for the mere reading of a gospel in churches on Sunday does not prove that it was considered divinely authoritative; and the use of the epistles, which formed the second and less valued part of the collection, must still have been limited.

Justin's disciple, Tatian (160-180 A.D.), wrote a *Diatessaron* or harmony of the gospels, which began, according to Ephrem Syrus, with John i. 1; but our knowledge of it is uncertain. The author omitted the genealogies of Jesus and

[1] *Apolog.* i. 97, ed. Thirlby.

everything belonging to His Davidic descent. He seems also to have put into it particulars derived from extra-canonical sources such as the Gospel according to the Hebrews. Doubtless he was acquainted with Paul's writings, as statements made in them are quoted; but he dealt freely with them according to Eusebius, and even rejected several epistles, probably first and second Timothy.[1]

In Polycarp's epistle (about 160 A.D.), which is liable to strong suspicions of having been written after the death of the bishop,[2] there are reminiscences of the synoptic gospels; and most of Paul's epistles as well as 1 Peter were used by the writer. But the idea of canonical authority, or a peculiar inspiration belonging to these writings, is absent.

---

[1] *Hieronymi Prooem. in Epist. ad Titum.*

[2] Comp. chap. xii., where γραφαί is applied to the apostolic epistles; a title they did [not receive so early as the age of Polycarp. Zahn himself admits this.

The author of the second Clementine epistle (about 150-160) had not a New Testament canon made up of the four gospels and epistles. His *Scripture* was the Old Testament, to which is applied the epithet "the Books" or "the Bible;" and the words of Christ. "The Apostles" immediately subjoined to "the Books," does not mean the New Testament, or a special collection of the apostolic epistles, as has been supposed.[1] The preacher employed a gospel or gospels as *Scripture;* perhaps those of Matthew and Luke, not the whole documents, but the parts containing the words of Christ.[2] He also used the Gospel of the Egyptians as an authoritative document, and quoted his sources freely. With the Johannine writings he seems to have been unacquainted.[3]

Athenagoras of Athens wrote an apology addressed to Marcus Aurelius (176 A.D.) In it

[1] Chapter xiv. 2.   [2] Chapter ii. 4.

[3] See *Clementis Romani ad Corinthios quae dicuntur epistulae, ed. de Gebhardt et Harnack* 2., sec. 10, Prolegomena.

he uses written and unwritten tradition, testing all by the Old Testament which was his only authoritative canon. He makes no reference to the Christian documents, but adduces words of Jesus with the verb "he says." It is not clear whether he quoted from the Synoptics; perhaps the passages which are parallel to Matthew v. 44, 45, 46,[1] and Mark x. 6,[2] were taken from these; but the matter is somewhat uncertain. His treatise on the resurrection appeals to a passage in one of Paul's epistles.[3]

Dionysius of Corinth (170 A.D.) complains of the falsification of his writings, but consoles himself with the fact that the same is done to the "Scriptures of the Lord," *i.e.*, the gospels containing the Lord's words; or rather the two parts of the early collection, "the gospel" and "the apostle," together; which agrees best with the age and tenor of his letters.[4] If such be

---

[1] *Legat. pro Christ.* 11, 12.   [2] *Ibid.* 33.
[3] Chapter xviii.   [4] *Ap.* Euseb. H.E., iv. 23.

the meaning, the collection is put on a par with the Old Testament, and regarded as inspired.

In the second epistle of Peter (about A.D. 170) Paul's epistles are regarded as *Scripture* (iii. 16.) This seems to be the earliest example of the canonising of any New Testament portion. Here a brotherly recognition of the Gentile apostle and his productions takes the place of former opposition. A false interpretation of his epistles is even supposed to have induced a departure from primitive apostolic Christianity.

The letter of the churches at Vienne and Lyons (177 A.D.) has quotations from the epistles to the Romans, Philippians, 1 Timothy, 1 Peter, Acts, the gospels of Luke and John, the Apocalypse. The last is expressly called *Scripture*.[1] This shows a fusion of the two original tendencies, the Petrine and Pauline; and the formation of a Catholic church with a common canon of authority. Accordingly, the

[1] *Ap.* Euseb. H.E., v. 1, p. 144, ed. Bright.

two apostles, Peter and Paul, are mentioned together.

Theophilus of Antioch (180 A.D.) was familiar with the gospels and most of Paul's epistles, as also the Apocalypse. Passages are cited from Paul as "the divine word."[1] He ascribes the fourth gospel to John, calling him an inspired man, like the Old Testament prophets.[2] We also learn from Jerome that he commented on the gospels put together by way of harmony.[3]

The author of the epistle to Diognetus (about 200 A.D.) shows his acquaintance with the gospels and Paul's epistles; but he never cites the New Testament by way of proof. Words are introduced into his discourse, in passing and from memory.[4]

[1] θεῖος λόγος. *Ad Autolycum*, iii. 14, p. 1141, ed Migne.
[2] *Ibid.*, ii. 22.   [3] Epist. 151, ad Algasiam.
[4] See Overbeck's *Studien zur Geschichte der alten Kirche*, *Abhandlung* I., in which the date of the letter is brought down till after Constantine. Surely this is too late.

The conception of a Catholic *canon* was realized about the same time as that of a Catholic *church*. One hundred and seventy years from the coming of Christ elapsed before the collection assumed a form that carried with it the idea of *holy* and *inspired*.[1] The way in which it was done was by raising the apostolic writings higher and higher till they were of equal authority with the Old Testament, so that the church might have a rule of appeal. But by lifting the Christian productions up to the level of the old Jewish ones, injury was done to that living consciousness which feels the opposition between spirit and letter; the latter writings tacitly assuming or keeping the character of a perfect rule even as to form. The Old Testament was not brought down to the New; the New was raised to the Old. It is clear that the earliest church fathers did not

[1] Davidson's *Introduction to the Study of the New Testament*, vol. ii. p. 508, &c.

use the books of the New Testament as sacred documents clothed with divine authority, but followed for the most part, at least till the middle of the second century, apostolic tradition orally transmitted. They were not solicitous about a canon circumscribed within certain limits.

In the second half, then, of the second century there was a canon of the New Testament consisting of two parts called *the gospel*[1] and *the apostle*.[2] The first was complete, containing the four gospels alone; the second, which was incomplete, contained the Acts of the Apostles and epistles, *i.e.*, thirteen letters of Paul, one of Peter, one of John, and the Revelation. How and where this canon originated is uncertain. Its birthplace may have been Asia Minor, like Marcion's; but it may have grown about the same time in Asia Minor, Alexandria, and Western Africa. At all events, Irenæus,

[1] τὸ εὐαγγέλιον.   [2] ὁ ἀπόστολος.

Clement of Alexandria, and Tertullian agree in recognizing its existence.

Irenæus had a canon which he adopted as apostolic. In his view it was of binding force and authoritative. This contained the four gospels, the Acts, thirteen epistles of Paul, the first epistle of John, and the Revelation. He had also a sort of appendix or deutero-canon, which he highly esteemed without putting it on a par with the received collection, consisting of John's second epistle, the first of Peter, and the Shepherd of Hermas. The last he calls *Scripture*.[1] The epistle to the Hebrews, that of Jude, James's, second Peter, and third John he ignored.

Clement's collection was more extended than Irenæus'. His appendix or deutero-canon included the epistle to the Hebrews, 2 John, Jude, the Apocalypse of Peter, the Shepherd of Hermas, the Epistles of Clement and Barna-

[1] *Advers. Hæres.*, iv. 20, 2.

bas. He recognised no obligatory canon, distinct and of paramount authority. But he separated the New Testament writings by their traditionally apostolic character and the degree of importance attached to them. He did not attach the modern idea of *canonical* in opposition to *non-canonical*, either to the four gospels or any other part of the New Testament. Barnabas is cited as an apostle.[1] So is the Roman Clement.[2] The Shepherd of Hermas is spoken of as *divine*.[3] Thus the line of the Homologoumena is not marked off even to the same extent as in Irenæus.

Tertullian's canon consisted of the gospels, Acts, thirteen epistles of Paul, the Apocalypse, and 1 John. As an appendix he had the epistle to the Hebrews, that of Jude, the Shepherd of Hermas, 2 John probably, and 1 Peter. This deutero-canon was not regarded

---

[1] *Stromateis*, ii. 6, p. 965, ed. Migne.
[2] *Ibid.*, iv. 17, p. 1312.   [3] *Ibid.*, i. 29, p. 928.

as authoritative. No trace occurs in his works of James' epistle, 2 Peter, and 3 John. He used the Shepherd, calling it *Scripture*,[1] without implying, however, that he put it on a par with the usually acknowledged canonical writings; but after he became a Montanist, he repudiated it as the apocryphal Shepherd of adulterers, "put among the apocryphal and false by every council of the churches."[2] It was *not*, however, reckoned among the spurious and false writings, either at Rome or Carthage, in the time of Tertullian. It was merely placed outside the universally received works by the western churches of that day.

These three fathers did not fix the canon absolutely. Its limits were still unsettled. But they sanctioned most of the books now accepted as divine, putting some extra-canonical productions almost on the same level with the rest, if not in theory at least in practice.

---

[1] *De Oratione*, cap. 12. [2] *De Pudicitia*, cap. 10-20.

The canon of Muratori is a fragmentary list which was made towards the end of the 2d century (170 A.D.) Its birthplace is uncertain, though there are traces of Roman origin. Its translation from the Greek is assumed, but that is uncertain. It begins with the four gospels in the usual order, and proceeds to the Acts, thirteen epistles of Paul, the epistles of John, that of Jude, and the Apocalypse. The epistle to the Hebrews, 1 and 2 Peter, 1 John and James are not named. The Apocalypse of Peter is also mentioned, but as not universally received. Of the Shepherd of Hermas, it is stated that it may be read in the Church. The epistle "to the Laodiceans" may either be that to the Ephesians, which had such superscription in Marcion's canon, or less probably the supposititious epistle mentioned in the codex Boernerianus,[1] after that to Philemon, and often re-

[1] G. of St Paul's epistles, a MS. of the ninth century according to Tischendorf.

ferred to in the middle ages.[1] That "to the Alexandrians" is probably the epistle to the Hebrews; though this has been denied without sufficient reason. According to the usual punctuation, both are said to have been forged in Paul's name, an opinion which may have been entertained among Roman Christians about 170 A.D. The Epistle to the Hebrews was rejected in the west, and may have been thought a supposititious work in the interests of Paulinism, with some reason because of its internal character,[2] which is at least semi-Pauline, though its Judaistic basis is apparent. The story about the origin of the fourth gospel with its apostolic and episcopal attestation, evinces a desire to establish the authenticity of

---

[1] See Anger's *Ueber den Laodicener Brief,* 1843.

[2] *Fertur etiam ad Laudecences alia ad Alexandrinos Pauli nomine fincte ad hesem Marcionis et alia plura quæ in Catholicam ecclesiam recepi non potest.* Perhaps a comma should be put after *nomine,* and *fincte* joined to what follows, to the *alia plura* said to be forged in the interest of Marcion.

a work which had not obtained universal acceptance at the time.[1] It is difficult to make out the meaning in various places; and there is considerable diversity of opinion among expositors of the document.[2] In accord with these facts we find Serapion bishop of the church at Rhossus, in Cilicia,[3] allowing the public use of the gospel of Peter;[4] which shews that there was no exclusive gospel-canon at the end of the second century, at least in Syria. The present canon had not then pervaded the churches in general.

What is the result of an examination of the Christian literature belonging to the

---

[1] *Quarti evangeliorum Johannis ex discipulis cohortantibus condiscipulis et episcopis suis dixit conjejunate mihi odie triduo et quid cuique fuerit revelatum alterutrum nobis ennarremus eadem nocte revelatum Andreæ ex apostolis ut recogniscentibus cunctis Johannis suo nomine cuncta discriberet.*

[2] It is printed and largely commented on by Credner in his *Geschichte des neutestamentlichen Kanon* edited by Volkmar, p. 141, &c., and by Westcott *On the Canon*, Appendix C, p. 466. 2d edition. Many others have explained it; especially Hilgenfeld.

[3] About A.D. 190.   [4] *Euseb.* H. E. vi. 12.

second century? Is it that a canon was then fixed, separating some books from others by a line so clear, that those on one side of it were alone reckoned inspired, authoritative, of apostolic origin or sanction; while those on the other were considered uninspired, unauthoritative, without claim to apostolicity, unauthentic? Was the separation between them made on any clear principle of demarcation? It cannot be said so. The century witnessed no such fact, but merely the incipient efforts to bring it about. The discriminating process was begun, not completed. It was partly forced upon the prominent advocates of a policy which sought to consolidate the Jewish and Gentile-Christian parties, after the decline of their mutual antagonism, into a united church. They were glad to transfer the current belief in the infallible inspiration of the Old Testament, to selected Christian writings, as an effective means of defence against those whom they considered outside a new organisation—the Catholic Church.

The stichometrical list of the Old and New Testament Scriptures in the Latin of the Clermont MS. (D), was that *read* in the African Church in the 3rd century. It is peculiar. After the Pentateuch, Joshua, Judges, Ruth, and the historical books, follow Psalms, Proverbs, Ecclesiastes, Canticles, Wisdom, Sirach, the twelve minor prophets, the four greater; three books of the Macabbees, Judith, Esdras, Esther, Job, and Tobit. In the New Testament, the four gospels, Matthew, John, Mark, Luke, are succeeded by ten epistles of Paul, two of Peter, the epistle of James, three of John, and that of Jude. The epistle to the Hebrews (characterized as that of Barnabas), the Revelation of John, Acts of the Apostles; the Shepherd of Hermas, the Acts of Paul, the Revelation of Peter, follow. The last three constitute a sort of appendix; and the number of their verses is given. It is possible that the carelessness of a transcriber may have caused some of the singularities observable in this list; such as the omission of the epistles to the Philippians and Thessalonians; but the end shows a freer idea of books fit for reading than what was usual even at that early time in the African Church.[1]

In Syria a version of the New Testament for the use of the church was made early in the 3d century. This work, commonly called the Peshito, wants 2 Peter, 2 and 3 John, Jude, and the Apocalypse. It has, however, all the other books, including the epistle of James and that to the Hebrews. The last two were received as apostolic.

Towards the middle of the 3rd century Origen's[2] testimony respecting the Canon is of great value. He seems to have distinguished three classes of books—authentic ones, whose apostolic origin was generally admitted, those

[1] Tischendorf edited the Pauline epistles from this MS. Lipsiæ, 1852.   [2] † 254 A.D.

not authentic, and a middle-class not generally recognised - or in regard to which his own opinion wavered. The first contained those already adopted at the beginning of the century both in the East and West, with the Apocalypse, and the epistle to the Hebrews *so far as it contains Pauline ideas;*[1] to the second belongs the Shepherd of Hermas, though he sometimes hesitated a little about it,[2] the epistle of Barnabas, the Acts of Paul, the gospel according to the Hebrews, the gospel of the Egyptians, and the preaching of Peter;[3] to the third, the epistle of James, that of Jude, 2 Peter, 2 and 3 John.[4] The separation of the various writings is not formally made, nor does Origen give a list of them. His classification is gathered from his works; and though its application admitted of considerable latitude, he is cautious enough,

[1] τὰ ἐν τῇ διαθήκῃ βιβλία, ἐνδιάθηκα, ὁμολογούμενα.

[2] In one place, however, he calls it *very useful and divinely inspired.* Comment. in ep. ad Roman., xvi. 14.   [3] νόθα.

[4] Ap. Euseb. *Hist. Eccles.*, vi. 25 ; iii. 25, ἀντιλεγόμενα.

appealing to the tradition of the church, and throwing in qualifying expressions.[1]

The Canon of Eusebius[2] is given at length in his *Ecclesiastical History*.[3] He divides the books into three classes, containing those writings *generally received*,[4] those *controverted*,[5] and the *heretical*.[6] The first has the four gospels, the Acts, thirteen epistles of Paul, 1 John, 1 Peter, the Apocalypse.[7] The second class is subdivided into two, the first corresponding to Origen's *mixed*[8] or *intermediate*

---

[1] See Euseb., *H. E.*, vi. 25. *Comment. in Matth.*, iii. p. 463; Ibid., p. 814; *Comment. in ep. ad Roman.*, iv. p. 683; *in Matth.*, iii. p. 644; *Homil.* viii. *in Numb.*, ii. p. 294; *Contra Cels.*, i. 63, p. 378; *De Principiis præf.*, i. p. 49. *Opp.*, ed. Delarue.

[2] † 340 A.D.

[3] *Hist. Eccles.*, iii. 25; also 31, 39; vi. 13, 14.

[4] ὁμολογούμενα, ἐνδιάθηκα, ἀναμφίλεκτα, ἀναντίρρητα.

[5] ἀντιλεγόμενα, γνώριμα δὲ τοῖς πολλοῖς, ἐν πλείσταις ἐκκλησίαις δεδημοσιευμένα, νόθα.

[6] ἄτοπα πάντη καὶ δυσσεβῆ; παντελῶς νόθα (iii. 31).

[7] This last with the qualification εἴγε φανείη. In another place he states that it was rejected by some, and therefore it is also along with the ἀντιλεγόμενα or νόθα.   [8] μικτά.

writings, the second to his *spurious*[1] ones. The former subdivision contains the epistle of James, 2 Peter, Jude, 2 and 3 John; the latter, the Acts of Paul, the Shepherd, the Revelation of Peter, the epistle of Barnabas, the Doctrines of the Apostles, the Apocalypse of John, the gospel according to the Hebrews. The third class has the gospels of Peter, of Thomas, the traditions of Matthias, the Acts of Peter, Andrew, and John. The subdivisions of the second class are indefinite. The only distinction which Eusebius puts between them is that of ecclesiastical use. Though he classes as *spurious* the Acts of Paul, the Shepherd, the Revelation of Peter, the epistle of Barnabas, the doctrines of the Apostles, the Apocalypse of John, the gospel according to the Hebrews, and does not apply the epithet to the epistle of James, the 2 of Peter, 2 and 3 John; he uses of James's in one place the verb *to be counted spuri-*

[1] νόθα.

ous.[1] In like manner he speaks of the Apocalypse of Peter and the epistle of Barnabas as *controverted*. The *mixed* or *spurious* of Origen are vaguely separated by Eusebius; both come under the general head of the *controverted*; for after specifying them separately he sums up, " all these will belong to the class of the *controverted*," the very class already described as containing " books well known and recognized by most," implying also that they were read in the churches.[3]

It is somewhat remarkable that Eusebius does not mention the Epistle of Clement to the Corinthians in this list. But he speaks of it in another place as a production whose authen-

---

[1] νοθεύομαι. *Hist. Eccles.*, ii. 23. Christophorson, Schmid, and Hug think that Eusebius gave the opinion of others in this word; but it is more likely that he gave his own, as Valesius thinks. See the note in Schmid's *Historia antiqua et vindicatio Canonis, &c.*, p. 358.

[2] *Ibid.*, vi. 14.

[3] See Weber's *Beiträge zur Geschichte des neutestamentlichen Kanons*, p. 142, &c.

ticity was generally acknowledged,[1] and of its public use in most churches both formerly and in his own time. This wide-spread reading of it did not *necessarily* imply canonicity; but the mode in which Eusebius characterises it, and its extensive use in public, favour the idea that in many churches it was almost put on equality with the productions commonly regarded as authoritative. The canonical list was not fixed immovably in the time of Eusebius. Opinions about books varied, as they had done before.

The testimony of Eusebius regarding the canon, important as it is, has less weight because of the historian's credulity. One who believed in the authenticity of Abgar's letters to Christ, and in the canon of the four gospels at the time of Trajan, cannot take rank as a judicious collector or sifter of facts.

About 332 A.D. the Emperor Constantine entrusted Eusebius with the commission to

[1] ὁμολογουμένη. *Hist. Eccles.*, iii. 16.

make out a complete collection of the sacred Christian writings for the use of the Catholic Church. How this order was executed we are not told. But Credner is probably correct in saying that the code consisted of all that is now in the New Testament except the Revelation. The fifty copies which were made must have supplied Constantinople and the Greek Church for a considerable time with an authoritative canon.

Eusebius's catalogue agrees in substance with that of Origen. The historian followed ecclesiastical tradition. He inquired diligently into the prevailing opinions of the Christian churches and writers, with the views held by others before and contemporaneously with himself, but could not attain to a decided result. His hesitation stood in the way of a clear, firm, view of the question. The tradition respecting certain books was still wavering, and he was unable to fix it. Authority fettered his independent judgment. That he was inconsistent and confused does not need to be shown.

The exact principles that guided the formation of a canon in the earliest centuries cannot be discovered. Strictly speaking there were none. Definite grounds for the reception or rejection of books were not apprehended. The choice was determined by various circumstances, of which apostolic origin was the chief, though this itself was insufficiently attested; for if it be asked whether all the New Testament writings proceeded from the authors whose names they bear, criticism cannot reply in the affirmative. The example and influence of churches to which the writings had been first addressed must have acted upon the reception of books. Above all, individual teachers here and there saw the necessity of meeting heretics with their own weapons, in their own way, with *apostolic records* instead of oral tradition. The circumstances in which the orthodox were placed led to this step, effecting a bond of union whose need must have been felt while each church was isolated under its own bishop and the collective body could not take measures in common. Writings of more recent origin would be received with greater facility than such as had been in circulation for many years, especially if they professed to come from a prominent apostle. A code of apostolic writings, divine and perfect like the Old Testament, had to be presented as soon as possible against Gnostic and Manichæan heretics whose doctrines were injurious to objective Christianity; while the multiplication of apocryphal works threatened to overwhelm genuine tradition with a heap of superstition. The Petrine and Pauline Christians, now amalgamated to a great extent, agreed in hastening the canon-process.

The infancy of the canon was cradled in an uncritical age, and rocked with traditional ease. Conscientious care was not directed from the first to the well-authenticated testimony of eye-witnesses. Of the three fathers who contributed most to its early growth, Irenæus was credulous and blundering; Tertullian passionate and one-sided; and Clement of Alexandria, imbued with the treasures of Greek wisdom, was mainly occupied with ecclesiastical ethics. Irenæus argues that the gospels should be four in number, neither more nor less, because there are four universal winds and four quarters of the world. The Word or Architect of all things gave the gospel in a fourfold shape. According to this father, the apostles were fully informed concerning all things, and had a perfect knowledge, after their Lord's ascension. Matthew wrote his gospel while Peter and Paul were preaching in Rome and founding the church.[1] Such assertions shew both ignorance and exaggeration.

Tertullian affirms that the *tradition of the*

[1] *Adversus Hæres*, iii., 11, 8.

apostolic churches guarantees the four gospels,[1] and refers his readers to the churches of Corinth, Philippi, Ephesus, &c., for the *authentic epistles* of Paul.[2] What is this but the rhetoric of an enthusiast? In like manner he states that bishops were appointed by the apostles, and that they existed from that time downward, the succession originating so early.[3]

Clement contradicts himself in making Peter authorise Mark's gospel to be read in the churches; while in another place he says that the apostle neither "forbad nor encouraged it."[4]

The three fathers of whom we are speaking, had neither the ability nor the inclination to examine the genesis of documents surrounded with an apostolic halo. No analysis of their authenticity and genuineness was seriously

---

[1] *Adv. Marc.* iv. 5. [2] *De præscript. hæret.* c. 36.
[3] *De praescript. haeret.* c. 32.
[4] *Ap. Euseb. Hist. Eccles.* ii. 15 and vi. 14.

attempted either by them or by the men of their time. In its absence custom, accident, taste, practical needs directed the tendency of tradition. All the rhetoric employed to throw the value of their testimony as far back as possible, even up to or at least very near the apostle John is of the vaguest sort. Appeals to the continuity of tradition and of church doctrine, to the exceptional veneration of these fathers for the gospels, to their opinions being formed earlier than the composition of the works in which they are expressed, possess no force. The ends which the fathers in question had in view, their polemic motives, their uncritical, inconsistent assertions, their want of sure data, detract from their testimony. Their decisions were much more the result of pious feeling biassed by the theological speculations of the times, than the conclusions of a sound judgment. The very arguments they use to establish certain conclusions shew weakness of perception. What are the manifestations of spiritual feeling, compared with the results of logical reasoning? Are they more trustworthy than the latter? Certainly not, at least in relation to questions of evidence. It is true that their testimony has a value; but it is one proportionate to the degree of credibility attaching to witnesses circumstanced as they were, whose separation of canonical from uncanonical gospels, or rather their canonising of certain writings apart from others, and their claiming of inspiration for the authors of the former, must be judged by the reasonableness of the thing itself, in connexion with men of their type. The second century abounded in pseudonymous literature; and the early fathers, as well as the churches, were occupied with other things than the sifting of evidence connected with writings considerably prior to their own time. The increase of such apocryphal productions, gospels, acts, and apocalypses among the heretical parties stimulated the orthodox bishops and churches to make an authentic collection; but it increased the difficulties of the task.

Textual criticism has been employed to discredit the true dates of the present gospels; and the most exaggerated descriptions have been given of the frequent transcription of the text and its great corruption in the second century. The process of corruption in the course of frequent transcription has been transferred even to the first century. It is true that the gospels at the end of that century exhibited a text which bears marks of transcription, interpolation, and addition; but they were not the complete works as we have them now, being then but in progress, except the fourth. The assumption that " advanced corruption" existed in the present text of the synoptists as early as the first century is gratuitous; unless the process by which they were gradually built up is so called.

No attempt to get a long history behind the canonical gospels at the close of the first century out of "advanced corruption" can be successful. It is attested by no Christian writer of the century; and those in the first half of the second, both heretical and orthodox, did themselves treat the text in a manner far short of its implied infallibility. The various readings with which they had to do, do not carry up *the canonical gospels* far into the first century. The transcription, enlargement, and interpolation of the materials which make up the body of them, must not be identified with the corruption of their *completed texts*, in order that the latter may be relegated to an early period; for the synoptists did not come forth full-blown, each from the hand of a single person. The old Latin version or versions used by Tertullian and the interpreter of Irenæus, have been pressed into the same service, but in vain.

In like manner the Curetonian Syriac version of the gospels has been put as early as possible into the second century, though it can hardly have been prior to the very close of it, or rather to the beginning of the third. Here the strong assertions of apologetic writers have been freely scattered abroad. But the evidence in favour of the authors traditionally assigned to the gospels and some of the epistles, is still uncertain. A wide gap intervenes between eye-witnesses of the apostles or apostolic men that wrote the sacred books, and the earliest fathers who assert such authorship. The traditional bridge between them is a precarious one. As the chasm cannot be filled by adequate external evidence, we are thrown back on the internal character of the works themselves. One thing appears from the early corruption of the sacred records spoken of by Irenæus, Origen, and others, that they were not regarded with the veneration necessarily attaching to infallible documents. Their being freely handled excludes the idea of rigid canonisation. The men who first canonised them had no certain knowledge of their authors. To them, that knowledge had been obscured or lost; though a sagacious criticism might have arrived at the true state of the question even in their day.

In the sub-apostolic age Ebionitism passed into Catholicism, Jewish into Pauline Christianity, the mythical and marvellous into the dogmatic, the traditional into the historic, the legendary into the literary. The conflict of parties within the sphere of Christianity gave rise to productions of various tendencies which reflected the circumstances out of which they arose. These were accepted or rejected by the churches according to the prevailing opinions of the persons composing the churches. Common usage led to the authorisation of some; others were neglected. The state of the second century in its beliefs, credulity, idiosyncracies of prominent teachers, antagonistic opinions and mystic speculations, throws a light upon the New Testament writings and especially on the formation of the canon, which explains their genesis. Two things stand out most clearly, the comparatively late idea of a *canonical* New Testament literature; and the absence of critical principles in determining it. The former was not entertained till the latter part of the second century. The conception of canonicity and inspiration attaching to New Testament books did not exist till the time of Irenæus.

When it is asked, to whom do we owe the canon? the usual answer is, to the Church. This is true only in a sense. The unity attributed to Christians before Irenæus and Tertullian, consisted in their religious consciousness. It was subjective. The idea of *the church* was that of inward fellowship,—the fellowship of the spirit rather than an outward organism. The preservation of the early Christian writings was owing, in the first instance, to the congregations to whom they were sent, and the neighbouring ones with whom such congregations had friendly connection. The care of them devolved on the most influential teachers,— on those who occupied leading positions in the chief cities, or were most interested in apostolic writings as a source of instruction. The Christian books were mostly in the hands of the bishops. In process of time the canon was the care of assemblies or councils. But it had been made before the first general council by a few leading fathers towards the end of the second century in different countries. The formation of a Catholic Church and of a canon was simultaneous. The circumstances in which the collection originated were unfavourable to the authenticity of its materials, for tradition had been busy over them and their authors. Instead of attributing the formation of the canon to the Church, it would be more correct to say that the important stage in it was due to three teachers, each working separately and in his own way, who were intent upon the creation of a Christian society which did not appear in the apostolic age,—a visible organisation united in faith,—where the discordant opinions of apostolic and sub-apostolic times should be finally merged. The canon was not the work of the Christian Church so much as of the men who were striving to form that Church, and could not get beyond the mould received by primitive Christian literature. The first mention of a *Catholic Church* occurs in *The Martyrdom of Polycarp*, an epistle that cannot be dated earlier than 160 A.D., and may perhaps be ten years later. But though the idea is there, its established use is due to Irenæus, Tertullian, and Cyprian. The expression has a different and narrow sense in the seven Ignatian epistles which we believe to be supposititious and later than Justin. Neither the three epistles published in Syriac by Cureton, nor the seven Greek ones enumerated by Eusebius are authentic; though Zahn has tried to prove the latter such, dating them A.D. 144. His arguments, however, are far from convincing; and the whole story of [1] Ignatius's martyrdom at Rome rather than Antioch is still doubtful; for the circumstances under which he is said to have been dragged to Rome, and his writing letters to the churches by the way, are highly improbable. The testimony of Malalas that Ignatius suffered at Antioch in December 115 in the presence of Trajan, may be quite as good as that of Chrysostom and the Syriac monthly calendar on which Zahn relies so con-

[1] *Ignatius von Antiochien*, 1873; and Prolegomena to the *Patrum Apostolicorum opera*, by de Gebhardt, Harnack, and Zahn, Fasciculus, ii.

fidently. The fact of the priority of the last two to Malalas is of little weight as evidence. The main point is *the locality* in which Ignatius suffered; which Malalas, himself a native of Antioch and a historian, ought to have known better than Chrysostom, because he copied preceding historians.

It is necessary to be precise on this subject because some speak of *the church* as though it were contemporary with the apostles themselves, or at least with their immediate disciples; and proceed to argue that dissensions arose soon after "within the church" rendering an appeal to the written word necessary. When the authority of *traditional teaching* gave way to that of *a written rule*, a change came over the condition of *the church*. Such a view tends to mislead. There were dissensions among the earliest Christians. The apostles themselves were by no means unanimous. Important differences of belief divided the Jewish and

Gentile Christians from the beginning. The types of Christian truth existing from the first gradually coalesced about the middle of the second century; when heretics, especially the Gnostics, appeared so formidable that a catholic church was developed. Along with this process, and as an important element in it, the writings of apostles and apostolic men were uncritically taken from tradition and elevated to the rank of divine documents. It was not the rise of new dissensions "within the church" which led to the first formation of a Christian canon; rather did the new idea of "a catholic church" require a standard of appeal in apostolic writings, which were now invested with an authority that did not belong to them from the beginning.

Origen was the first who took a somewhat scientific view of the relative value belonging to the different parts of the biblical collection. His examination of the canon was critical.

Before him the leading books had been regarded as divine and sacred, the source of doctrinal and historic truth. From this stand-point he did not depart. With him ecclesiastical tradition was a prevailing principle in the recognition of books belonging of right to the New Testament collection. He was also guided by the inspiration of the authors ; a criterion arbitrary in its application, as his own statements show. In his time, however, the collection was being gradually enlarged ; his third class, *i.e., the mixed*, approaching reception into the first. But amid all the fluctuations of opinion to which certain portions of the New Testament were subject, and the unscientific procedure both of fathers and churches in the matter, though councils had not met to discuss it, and vague tradition had strengthened with time, a certain spiritual consciousness manifested itself throughout the East and West in the matter of the canon. Tolerable unanimity ensued.

The result was a remarkable one, and calls for our gratitude, notwithstanding its defects. Though the development was pervaded by no critical or definite principle, it ended in a canon which has maintained its validity for centuries.

It is sometimes said that the history of the canon should be sought from definite catalogues, not from isolated quotations. The latter are supposed to be of slight value, the former to be the result of deliberate judgment. This remark is more specious than solid. In relation to the Old Testament, the catalogues given by the fathers, as by Melito and Origen, rest solely on the tradition of the Jews; apart from which they have no independent authority. As none except Jerome and Origen knew Hebrew, their lists of the Old Testament books are simply a reflexion of what they learned from others. If they deviate in practice from their masters by quoting as Scripture other than the canonical books, they show their judgment over-riding an external theory. The very men who give a list of the Jewish books evince an inclination to the Christian and enlarged canon. So Origen says, in his *Epistle to Africanus*, that "the churches use Tobit." In explaining the prophet Isaiah, Jerome employs Sirach vi. 6, in proof of his view, remarking that the apocryphal work is in the Christian catalogue. In like manner Epiphanius, in a passage against Aetius, after referring to the books of Scripture, adds, "as well as the books of Wisdom, *i.e.*, the Wisdom of Solomon and of Jesus son of Sirach; finally, all the other books of Scripture." In another place he gives the canon of the Jews historically, and excludes the apocryphal Greek books; here he includes some of the latter. We also learn from Jerome that Judith was in the number of the books reckoned up by the Nicene Council. Thus the fathers who give catalogues of the Old Testament shew the existence of a Jewish and a Christian canon in relation to the Old Testament; the latter wider than the former; their private opinion being more favourable to the one, though the other was historically transmitted. In relation to the New Testament, the synods which drew up lists of the sacred books show the view of some leading father like Augustine, along with what custom had sanctioned. In this department no member of the synod exercised his critical faculty; a number together would decide such questions summarily. Bishops proceed in the track of tradition or authority.

CHAPTER VII.

THE BIBLE CANON FROM THE FOURTH CENTURY TO THE REFORMATION.

IT will now be convenient to treat of the two Testaments together, *i.e., the canon of the Bible.* The canons of both have been considered separately to the end of the third century; they may be henceforward discussed together. We proceed, therefore, to the Bible-canon of the fourth century, first in the Greek Church and then in the Latin. The Council of Laodicea (A.D. 363), at which there was a predominant semiarian influence, forbad the reading of all *non-canonical* books. The 59th canon enacts, that "private psalms must not be read in the Church, nor uncanonized books; but only the canonical ones of the New and Old Testament." The 60th canon proceeds to give a list of such. All the books of the Old Testament are enumerated, but in a peculiar order, somewhat like the Septuagint one. With Jeremiah is specified *Baruch*, then the Lamentations and *Epistle*. The prophets are last; first the minor, next the major and Daniel. In the New Testament list are the usual seven Catholic epistles, and fourteen of Paul including that to the Hebrews. The Apocalypse alone is wanting. Credner has proved that this 60th canon is not original, and of much later date.[1]

The Apostolic Constitutions give a kind of canon like that in the 59th of Laodicea. After speaking of the books of Moses, Joshua, Judges Kings, Chronicles, those belonging to the return from the captivity, those of Job, Solomon, the sixteen prophets, and the Psalms of David; our Acts, the epistles of Paul, and the four

[1] *Geschichte des neutest. Kanon*, p. 217, &c.

gospels are mentioned. It is remarkable that the Catholic epistles are not given. That they are indicated under Acts is altogether improbable. The Antiochian Church of that time doubted or denied the apostolicity of these letters, as is seen from Theodore, Cosmas, and others. Hence their absence from these Constitutions, which are a collection belonging to different times; the oldest portion not earlier perhaps than the third century.[1]

Cyril of Jerusalem, who took part in the Council of Laodicea,[2] gives a list "of the divine Scriptures." The books of the Old Testament are twenty-two, and the arrangement is nearly that which is in the English Bible. With Jeremiah is associated "Baruch and the Epistle." All the New Testament books are given except the Apocalypse. The list agrees very nearly with that of Eusebius, by taking the latter's "controverted" writings into the class of the

[1] See *Constit. Apostol.*, p. 67, ed. Ueltzen.   [2] † 386 A.D.

"generally received."[1] The writer insists on the necessity of unity in the Church upon the subject, and forbids the reading of writings not *generally received.* None but these are allowed. Yet he refers to Baruch (iii. 36-38) as *the prophet;*[2] and in adducing the testimonies of the prophets for the existence of the Holy Spirit, the last he gives is Daniel xiii. 41, 45. Sirach iii. 21, 22 is cited;[3] Wisdom is quoted as Solomon's (xiii. 5);[4] the song of the three children is used (verse 55)[5] with verses 27, 29;[6] and Daniel (xiii. 22, 45) is quoted.[7]

In Athanasius's festal epistle (365 A.D.) the archbishop undertakes "to set forth in order the books that are canonical and handed down and believed to be divine." His list of the Old Testament nearly agrees with Cyril's, except that Esther is omitted and Ruth

---

[1] *Catech.*, iv. 22, pp. 66, 67, ed. Milles.
[2] *Ibid.*, xi. p. 142.
[3] *Ibid.*, vi. p. 80.
[4] *Ibid.*, ix. pp. 115, 122.
[5] *Ibid.*, ix. p. 115.
[6] *Ibid.*, ii. p. 31.
[7] *Ibid.*, xvi. p. 239.

counted separately, to make out the twenty-two books. He adds, "there are other books not canonical, designed by the fathers to be read by those just joining us and wishing to be instructed in the doctrine of piety;" *i.e.*, the Wisdom of Solomon and the Wisdom of Sirach, and Esther and Judith and Tobit, and the Doctrine of the Apostles so called, and the Shepherd; "those being *canonical*, and these being *read*, let there be no mention of apocryphal writings," &c. The New Testament list is the same as Cyril's, with the addition of the Apocalypse.[1] He quotes several of the apocryphal books in the same way as he does the canonical. Thus he introduces Judith (viii. 16) with "the Scripture said;"[2] and Baruch (iii. 12) is cited as if it were Scripture.[3] Wisdom (vi. 26) has the epithet Scripture applied to it.[4] Sirach (xv. 9) is intro-

---

[1] Athanasii *Opp.* ed. Benedict. i. 2, pp. 962, 963.
[2] *Orat. contra Arianos*, ii. 35, vol. i. 503, ed. Benedict.
[3] *Ibid.*, ii. 42, i. p. 510. [4] *Ibid.*, ii. 79, i. p. 546.

duced with "what is said by the Holy Spirit." Baruch (iv. 20, 22) and Daniel (xiii. 42) are referred to in the same way as Isaiah.[2] Tobit (ii. 7) has "it is written" prefixed to it.[3] Canonical and apocryphal are mentioned together; and similar language applied to them.

Eusebius of Caesarea cites Wisdom as a *divine oracle;*[4] and after adducing several passages from Proverbs, subjoining to them others from the same book with the introductory formula "these are also said to be the same writers," he concludes with "such is the scripture."[5] Sirach is cited as Solomon's along with various passages from Proverbs.[6] After quoting Baruch, he says, "there is no need to appeal to the divine voices, which clearly confirm our proposition."[7] The additions to Daniel are also treated as Scripture.[8]

[1] *Epist. ad episcop. Ægypt.*, &c., i. 1, p. 272.
[2] *Contra Arian.*, i. 12, i. p. 416.
[3] *Apolog. contra Arianos*, ii., vol. i. p. 133.
[4] *Praepar. Evan.*, i. 9.   [5] *Ibid.*, xi. 14.   [6] *Ibid.*, xii. 18.
[7] *Ibid.*, vi. 11.   [8] *Demon. Evang.*, vi. 19.

Basil of Caesarea[1] had a canon agreeing with that of Athanasius. Along with the usual books reckoned as belonging to the canon, he used the apocryphal productions of the Old Testament. Thus the book of Wisdom (i. 4)[2] is quoted by him. So are Sirach (xx. 2);[3] Baruch, (iii. 36)[4] called Jeremiah's; Judith (ix. 4);[5] and Daniel (xiii. 50).[6]

Gregory of Nazianzus[7] puts his list into a poetical form. In the Old Testament it agrees with Athanasius's exactly, except that he mentions none but the canonical books. Like Athanasius, he omits Esther. In the New Testament he deviates from Athanasius, by leaving out the Apocalypse, which he puts among the spurious.[8] He does not ignore the apocryphal

---

[1] † 379 A.D.

[2] *Homil. in princip. proverb. Opp.* ed. Garnier altera, vol. ii. p. 140.   [3] *Constitutiones Monast.*, c. iii. 2. *Ibid.*, p. 779.

[4] *Adv. Eunom,* vol. i. p. 417.

[5] *De Spiritu Sancto,* c. viii. vol. iii. p. 23.

[6] *In Princip. Proverb,* vol. ii. p. 152.   [7] † 389 A.D.

[8] *Opp.* ed. Migne, vol. iii. pp. 473, 474.

books of the Old Testament, but quotes Daniel xiii. 5.[1]

Amphilochius of Iconium[2] gives a metrical catalogue of the Biblical books. The canon of the old Testament is the usual one, except that he says of Esther at the end, "some judge that Esther should be added to the foregoing." He notices none of the apocryphal books. His New Testament canon agrees with the present, only he excludes the Apocalypse as *spurious;* which is given as the judgment of the majority. He alludes to the doubts that existed as to the epistle to the Hebrews, but regards it as Pauline; and to the number of the catholic epistles (seven or three).[3] The concluding words show that no list was universally received at that time.

Epiphanius[4] follows Athanasius in his canon.

---

[1] Gregorii Nazianzeni, *Opp.* ed. Migne, vol. iii. pp. 473, 474.
[2] † 395 A.D.
[3] Iambi ad Seleucum; in Greg. Naz. *Opp.* ii. p. 194.
[4] † 403 A.D.

As to the number of the Old Testament books, he hesitates between twenty-two and twenty-seven; but the contents are the same. At the end of the twenty-seven books of the New Testament, Wisdom and Sirach are mentioned as "divine writings;" elsewhere they are characterized as "doubtful."[1] His practice shows his sentiments clearly enough, when Sirach (vii. 1) is introduced with "the Scripture" testifies[2]; vii. 9 is elsewhere quoted[3]; Wisdom (i. 4) is cited as Solomon's[4]; Baruch (iii. 36) is introduced with, "as the Scripture says,[5]" and Daniel (xiii. 42) is quoted with, "as it is written."[6] He mentions the fact that the epistles of Clement of Rome were read in the churches.[7]

---

[1] ἀμφιλέκτα. *Adv. Hæres*, i. p. 19. See *Hæres*, iii. tom. i. p. 941. De ponder. et mensur. 23.
[2] *Advers. Hæres*, lib. i., tom. 2 ed. Petav. Paris, 1662, p. 72.
[3] *Ibid.*, lib. ii. tom. ii. p. 781. [4] *Ibid.*, lib. ii. tom. i. p. 580.
[5] *Ibid.*, lib. ii. tom. i. p. 481. [6] *Ibid.*, lib. i. tom. ii. p. 157.
[7] *Hæres*, xxx. 15.

Didymus of Alexandria[1] speaks against 2 Peter that it is not in the canons.[2]

Chrysostom[3] does not speak of the canon; but in the New Testament he never quotes the last four catholic epistles or the Apocalypse. All the other parts he uses throughout his numerous works,[4] including the Apocrypha. Thus he introduces Wisdom (xvi. 28) with "Scripture says.[5]" He quotes Baruch (iii. 36, 38)[6]; and Sirach (iv. 1).[7]

Didymus of Alexandria[8] cites Baruch (iii. 35) as Jeremiah,[9] and treats it like the Psalms.[10]

---

[1] † 392 A.D.

[2] Enarrat. in ep. S. Petri secundam, p. 1774 ed. Migne.

[3] † 407 A.D.

[4] See Montfaucon in his edition of Chrysostom's Works, vol. vi. pp. 364, 365, ed. Paris, 1835.

[5] Expos. in Psalm cix. 7. See also xi. 1 in Genes, where Wisdom xiv. 3 is cited.

[6] Expos. in Psalm xlix. 3.

[7] De Lazaro, ii. 4. [8] † 392 A.D.

[9] De Trinitate, iii. 2. p. 792 ed. Migne.

[10] Fragmenta in Epist. 2 ad Corinthios, when Baruch, iii. 3, is quoted like Psalm 101, p. 1697.

Daniel (xiii. 45) is also quoted.[1] He says of Peter's Second Epistle that it is not in the canon.

Theodore of Mopsuestia[2] was much freer than his contemporaries in dealing with the books of Scripture. It seems that he rejected Job, Canticles, Chronicles, and the Psalm-inscriptions; in the New Testament the epistle of James, and others of the catholic ones. But Leontius's account of his opinions cannot be adopted without suspicion.[3]

The canon of Cyril of Alexandria[4] does not differ from Athanasius's. Like other writers of the Greek Church in his day he uses along with the canonical the apocryphal books of the Old Testament. He quotes 1 (iii.) Edras (iv. 36) with "inspired Scripture says."[5] Wisdom (vii. 6) is introduced with, "according to that which

---

[1] De Spirit. sanct. i. p. 1033.   [2] † 428 A.D.

[3] See Leontius Byzantinus contra Nestorianos et Eutychianos, lib. iii. in *Gallandi Bibliotheca*, xii. p. 690. Comp. Fritzsche *De Theodori Mopsuesteni vita et scriptis*, Halæ, 1836.

[4] † 444 A.D.   [5] Contra Julian. i. p. 541, ed. Migne.

is written."[1] In another place it has the prefix
"for it is written" (i. 7);[2] and is treated as
Scripture (ii. 12).[3] Sirach (i. 1) is cited.[4]
Baruch also (iii. 35-37) is introduced with,
"another of the holy prophets said."[5]

The catalogues of the Old Testament contained in the manuscripts B, C, and א need not be given, as they are merely codices of the Septuagint, and have or had the books canonical and apocryphal belonging to that version. The list of the New Testament books in B is like that of Athanasius. Imperfect at the end, the MS. must have had at first the Epistles to Timothy, Titus, Philemon, and the Apocalypse. C (cod. Ephraemi rescriptus) has fragments of the New Testament, which show that it had originally all the present books in the same order as Athanasius's. א or the Sinaitic manuscript has

---

[1] *Ibid.*, p. 815.
[2] *Ibid.*, p. 921.
[3] In Isaim, ed. Migne, p. 93.
[4] P. 859, vol. i.
[5] P. 910, vol. i., ed. Migne.

the Epistle of Barnabas and the Shepherd of Hermas, in addition to the New Testament.

The progress made by the Greek Church of the fourth and former part of the fifth century, in its conception of the canon seems to be, that the idea of ecclesiastical settlement, or public, legal, definitive establishment was attached to the original one. A writing was considered canonical when a well-attested tradition put it among those composed by inspired men, apostles or others; and it had on that account a determining authority in matters of faith. Books which served as a rule of faith and were definitively set forth by the Church as divinely authoritative, were now termed *canonical.* The canon consisted of writings settled or determined by ecclesiastical law.[1] Such was the idea added to the original acceptation of canon. To canonical were opposed apocryphal writings, *i.e., heretical* and *fabricated* ones; while an

[1] βιβλία κανονιζόμενα, κανονικά, κεκανονισμένα, ὡρισμένα.

intermediate class consisted of those read in the churches, which were useful, but not decisive in matters of belief. Another advance in the matter of the canon at this period was the general adoption of the Hebrew canon, with a relegation of the Greek additions in the Septuagint to the class *publicly read*.[1] Yet doubts about the reception of Esther into the number of the canonical books were still entertained, though it was one of the Jewish canon; doubtless on account of its want of harmony with Christian consciousness. And the catholic epistles which had been doubted before, Jude, James, Second Peter, were now generally received. But there was a division of opinion about the Apocalypse.

We come to the period of the Latin corresponding to that of the Greek Church which has just been noticed. Augustine[2] gave great attention to the subject, labouring to establish a

---

[1] βιβλία ἀναγινωσκόμενα. [2] †430 A.D.

complete canon, the necessity of which was
generally felt. According to him the Scriptures
which were received and acknowledged by all
the churches of the day should be canonical,
Of those not universally adopted, such as are
received by the majority and the weightier of
the churches, should be preferred to those
received by the fewer and less important
churches. In his enumeration of the forty-
four books of the Old Testament, he gives,
after Chronicles, other histories "which are
neither connected with the order" specified in
the preceding context, "nor with one another,"
i.e., Job, Tobit, Esther, Judith, the two books of
the Maccabees, and Esdras. Wisdom and
Ecclesiasticus, he thinks, should be numbered
among the prophets, as deserving of authority
and having a certain likeness to Solomon's
writings.[1] He says of the Maccabees that this

---

[1] The forty-four books are, 5 of Moses, Joshua, Judges, Ruth, 4 Kings, 2 Chronicles, Job, Tobit, Esther, Judith, 2 Maccabees,

"Scripture has been received by the Church not uselessly, if it be read or heard soberly."[1] The famous passage in the treatise on Christian doctrine, where he enumerates the whole canon, is qualified by no other; for though he knew the distinction between the canonical books of the Palestinian Jews and the so-called apocryphal ones, as well as the fact of some New Testament writings not being received universally, he thought *church-reception* a sufficient warrant for canonical authority. Hence he considered the books of the Maccabees canonical, because so received by the Church; while he says of Wisdom and Sirach that they merited *authoritative* reception and numbering among the *prophetic* Scriptures.[2] Of the former in particular he speaks strongly in one place, asserting that it is worthy to be

Ezra, Nehemiah, Psalms, 3 of Solomon, Wisdom, Ecclesiasticus, 12 Prophets, 4 greater do. *De Doctrina Christiana* ii. 8.

[1] *Contra Gaudent.* i. 38; *Opp.* Paris, 1837, vol. ix. p. 1006.
[2] *De Doctr. Christ.* ii. 8. *Civitat. Dei.* xviii. 20, 1.

venerated by all Christians as of divine authority.[1] But he afterwards retracted his opinion of the canonical authority of Sirach.[2] He raises, not lowers, the authority of the so-called apocryphal books which he mentions. He enumerates all the New Testament books, specifying the Pauline epistles as fourteen, and so reckoning that to the Hebrews as the apostle's; but he speaks of it elsewhere as an epistle about which some were uncertain, professing that he was influenced to admit it as canonical by the authority of the Oriental churches.[3] In various places he speaks hesitatingly about its Pauline authorship.

In 393 the African bishops held a council at Hippo where the canon was discussed. The list of the canonical Scriptures given includes, besides the Palestinian one, Wisdom, Ecclesiasticus, Tobit, Judith, and the two books of

---

[1] *De Praedest. Sanct.* i. 11.   [2] *Retractt.* i. 10.
[3] *De peccat. merit.* i. 50; *Opp.* vol. x. p. 137, ed. Migne.

Maccabees. The New Testament canon seems to have agreed exactly with our present one.[1] The Council of Carthage (397) repeated the statute of its predecessor, enumerating the same books of the Bible as canonical.[2] Augustine was the animating spirit of both councils, so that they may be taken as expressing his views on the subject.

Jerome[3] gives a list of the twenty-two canonical books of the Old Testament, the same as that of the Palestinian Jews, remarking that some put Ruth and Lamentations among the Hagiographa, so making twenty-four books. All besides should be put among the Apocrypha. Wisdom, Sirach, Judith, Tobit, the Shepherd are not in the canon. The two books of Maccabees he regarded in the same light.[4] But though Jerome's words imply the apocry-

---

[1] *Mansi*, tom. iii. p. 924.   [2] *Ibid.*, p. 891.
[3] †420 A.D.
[4] *Prologus galeatus in Libros Regum. Epist. ad Paulinum.*

phal position of these extra-canonical books, he allows of their being read in public- for the edification of the people, not to confirm the authority of doctrines; *i.e.*, they belong to "the ecclesiastical books" of Athanasius. His idea of "apocryphal" is wider and milder than that of some others in the Latin Church. It has been conjectured by Welte,[1] that the conclusions of the African councils in 393 and 397 influenced Jerome's views of the canon, so that his later writings allude to the apocryphal works in a more favourable manner than that of the *Prologus galeatus* or the preface to Solomon's books. One thing is clear, that he quotes different passages from the Apocrypha along with others from the Hebrew canon. In his letter to Eustochius, Sirach iii. 33 (Latin) comes between citations from Matthew and Luke; and is introduced by *which is written*, in a letter to Pammachius; and xxii. 6 has *divine*

[1] In Herbst's *Einleit.*, *erster Theil*, p. 37.

Scripture applied to it.[1] Ruth, Esther, and Judith are spoken of as *holy volumes*. The practice of Jerome differed from his theory; or rather he became less positive, and altered his views somewhat with the progress of time and knowledge. As to the New Testament, he gives a catalogue of all that now belongs to it, remarking of the epistle to the Hebrews and of the Apocalypse that he adopts both on the authority of ancient writers, not of present custom. His opinion about them was not decided.[2] In another work he gives the Epistle of Barnabas at the end of the canonical list. He also states the doubts of many respecting the Epistle to Philemon, and about 2 Peter, Jude, 2 and 3 John. According to him the first Epistle of Clement of Rome was publicly read in some churches.[3]

[1] *Opp.* ed. Benedict., Vol. IV., pp. 679, 584, 750.
[2] Ep. ad Dardan. *Opp.* vol. i. p. 1103, ed. Migne.
[3] See *Onomastica Sacra;* Comment. in Ep. ad Philem; De Viris illustr.

Hilary of Poitiers[1] seems to have followed Origen's catalogue. . He gives twenty-two books, specifying "the epistle" of Jeremiah; and remarks that some added Tobit and Judith, making twenty-four, after the letters of the Greek alphabet. He cites Wisdom and Sirach as "prophets."[2] In the New Testament he never quotes James, Jude, 2 and 3 John, nor 2 Peter. 2 Maccabees (vii. 28) is introduced with "according to the prophet;"[3] Sirach (xxxi. 1) is introduced with "nor do they hear the Lord saying;"[4] Wisdom is cited as Solomon's (viii. 2);[5] Judith (xvi. 3) is cited;[6] so is Baruch (iii. 36);[7] and Daniel xiii. 42.[8]

Optatus of Mela[9] has the usual canonical books, but omits the epistle to the Hebrews.

[1] † 368 A.D.

[2] Prolog. in Psalm., *Opp.* ed. Migne, vol. i. p. 241.

[3] *De Trinitate* iv. 16.

[4] *Ex. Op. Hist. Fragmentum,* iii. vol. ii. p. 672, ed. Migne.

[5] In cxxvii. Psalm. [6] In Psalm cxxvi. 6.

[7] In Psalm lxviii. 19, and *De Trinitate,* iv. 42.

[8] *Ibid.,* iv. 8. [9] † About 370 A.D.

He uses the apocrypha without scruple, introducing Sirach (iii. 30) with "it is written;"[1] and Wisdom (i. 13) with "it is written in Solomon."[2]

Lucifer of Cagliari[3] uses the apocrypha equally with the canonical books. Thus 1 Maccabees (i. 43) is quoted as "holy Scripture."[4] So is 2 Maccab. (vi. 1).[5] Judith (ix. 2) is cited,[6] as are also Wisdom (xvii. 1, 2)[7]; Tobit (iv. 6);[8] and Daniel (xiii. 20).[9]

Ambrose of Milan[10] had the same canon as most of the Westerns in his time. With some others, he considered the Epistle to the Hebrews to have been written by St Paul. In the Old Testament he used the apocryphal books pretty freely. Wisdom (vii. 22) is cited

---

[1] *De Schismate Donatist.* iii. 3.
[2] *Ibid.*, ii. 25   [3] † about 370., A.D.
[4] *De non parcendo*, &c., ed. Coleti, p. 190.
[5] *Ibid.*, p. 236.   [6] *Ibid.*, p. 187.
[7] *Pro Athanasio*, lib. i. p. 98.   [8] *Ibid.*, p. 105.
[9] *Ibid.*, lib. ii. pp. 127, 128.   [10] † 397 A.D.

as authoritative Scripture.[1] Sirach (xi. 30) is also cited as Scripture.[2] Baruch (iv. 19) is quoted;[3] Daniel (xiii. 44, 45) is treated as Scripture and prophetic;[4] and Tobit is expounded like any other book of Scripture.[5]

Rufinus[6] enumerates the books of the Old and New Testaments which "are believed to be inspired by the Holy Spirit itself, according to the tradition of our ancestors, and have been handed down by the Churches of Christ." All the books of the Hebrew canon and of the New Testament are specified. After the list he says, "these are they which the fathers included in the canon, by which they wished to establish the assertion of our faith." He adds that there are other books not *canonical*, but *ecclesiastical*—the Wisdom of Solomon, Sirach, Tobit, Judith, and the books of the Maccabees.

---

[1] *De Spiritu Sancto* iii. 18. [2] *De bono mortis* viii.
[3] In Psalm cxviii., Sermo. 118, 2.
[4] *De Spirit. Sanct.* iii., vi. 39.
[5] *Liber de Tobia.* [6] †410 A.D.

Besides the usual New Testament works, he speaks of the Shepherd of Hermas, and the "Judgment of Peter" as read in the churches, but not as authoritative in matters of faith.[1]

Philastrius[2] of Brescia gives some account of the Scriptures and their contents in his time. The canonical Scriptures, which alone should be read in the Catholic Church, are said to be the law and the prophets, the gospels, Acts, thirteen epistles of Paul, and seven others, *i.e.*, two of Peter, three of John, one of Jude, and one of James. Of the Old Testament apocrypha he asserts that they ought to be read for the sake of morals by the perfect, but not by all. He speaks of *heretics* who reject John's gospel and the Apocalypse. Respecting the Epistle to the Hebrews which is omitted in his canon, he speaks at large, but not very decidedly, affirming that some attributed its authorship to

[1] *Expos. in Symbol. Apostol.*, pp. 373, 374, ed. Migne.
[2] †About 387 A.D.

Barnabas, or Clement of Rome, or Luke. "They wish to read the writings of the blessed apostle, and not rightly perceiving some things in the epistle, it is not therefore read by them in the church. Though read by some, it is not read to the people in the church; nothing but Paul's thirteen epistles, and that to the Hebrews sometimes."[1] The influence of the East upon the West appears in the statements of this father upon the subject. He had several canonical lists before him; one at least from an Oriental-Arian source, which explains some assertions, particularly his omission of the Apocalypse.

Innocent I. of Rome wrote to Exsuperius (405 A.D.), bishop of Toulouse, giving a list of the canonical books. Besides the Hebrew canon, he has Wisdom and Sirach; Tobit, Judith, the two Maccabees. The New Testament list is identical with the present. He also refers to

[1] De Hæres. chs. 60 and 61, in Galland, vii. pp. 424, 425.

pseudepigraphical writings which ought not only to be rejected but condemned.[1]

A canonical list appears in three different forms bearing the names of Damasus (366-384), Gelasius I. (492-496), and Hormisdas (514-523). According to the first, the books of the Old Testament are arranged in three orders. In the first are the Pentateuch, Joshua, Judges, Ruth, four Kings, two Chronicles, Psalms, Proverbs, Ecclesiastes, Canticles, Wisdom, and Ecclesiasticus; in the second, all the prophets, including Baruch; in the third, Job, Tobit, Judith, Esther, Esdras, two Maccabees. The New Testament books are the four gospels, fourteen epistles of Paul, the Apocalypse, and Acts, with seven Catholic epistles.

That which is called the Decree of Gelasius is almost identical with the preceding. It wants Baruch and Lamentations. It has also two Esdrases instead of one. In the New

[1] Apud Mansi, iii. pp. 1040, 1041.

Testament the epistle to the Hebrews is absent.

The Hormisdas-form has the Lamentations of Jeremiah: and in the New Testament the Epistle to the Hebrews.

The MSS. of these lists present some diversity; and Credner supposes the Damasus-list a fiction. But Thiel has vindicated its authenticity. It is possible that some interpolations may exist in the last two; the first, which is the shortest, may well belong to the time of Damasus.[1]

In 419 A.D. another council at Carthage, at which Augustine was present, repeated the former list of books with a single alteration, viz., fourteen epistles of Paul (instead of (thirteen).[2]

The preceding notices and catalogues show a general desire in the Western Church to settle

[1] Credner's *Zur Geschichte des Kanons*, p. 151, &c., and Thiel's *Epistolæ Romanorum Pontificum genuinae*, tom. i.

[2] Mansi iv. p. 430.

the canon. The two most influential men of the period were Augustine and Jerome, who did not entirely agree. Both were unfitted for a critical examination of the topic. The former was a gifted spiritual man, lacking learning and independence. Tradition dominated all his ideas about the difficult or disputed books. He did not enter upon the question scientifically, on the basis of certain principles; but was content to take refuge in authority—the prevailing authority of leading churches. His judgment was weak, his sagacity moderate, and his want of many-sidedness hindered a critical result. Jerome, again, was learned but timid, lacking the courage to face the question fairly or fundamentally; and the independence necessary to its right investigation. Belonging as he did to both churches, he recommended the practice of the one to the other. He, too, was chiefly influenced by tradition; by Jewish teachers in respect to the Old Testament, and by general custom as to the New. The question was not susceptible of advancement under such manipulation ; nor could it be settled on a legitimate basis. Compared with the eastern Church, the western accepted a wider canon 'of the Old Testament, taking some books into the class of the *canonical* which the former put among those *to be read*. In regard to the New Testament, *all* the Catholic epistles and even the Apocalypse were received. The African churches and councils generally adopted this larger canon, because the old Latin version or versions of the Bible current in Africa were daughters of the Septuagint. If the Latins apparently looked upon the Greek as the original itself, the apocryphal books would soon get rank with the canonical. Yet the more learned fathers, Jerome, Rufinus and others, favoured the Hebrew canon in distinguishing between *canonical* and *ecclesiastical* books. The influence of the Eastern upon the

Western Church is still visible, though it could not extinguish the prevailing desire to include the disputed books. The Greek view was to receive nothing which had not apparently a good attestation of divine origin and apostolic authority; the Latin was to exclude nothing hallowed by descent and proved by custom. The former Church looked more to the sources of doctrine; the latter to those of edification. The one desired to contract those sources, so as not to be too rich; the other to enlarge the springs of edification, not to be too poor. Neither had the proper resources for the work, nor a right perception of the way in which it should be set about; and therefore they were not fortunate in their conclusions, differing as they did in regard to points which affect the foundation of a satisfactory solution.

Notwithstanding the numerous endeavours both in the East and West to settle the canon during the 4th and 5th centuries, it was not finally closed. The doubts of individuals were still expressed; and succeeding ages testified to the want of universal agreement respecting several books. The question, however, was *practically* determined. No material change occurred again in the absolute rejection or admission of books. With some fluctuations, the canon remained very much as it was in the 4th and 5th centuries. Tradition shaped and established its character. General usage gave it a permanency which it was not easy to disturb. No definite principles guided the course of its formation, or fixed its present state. It was dominated first and last by circumstances and ideas which philosophy did not actuate. Its history is mainly objective. Uncritical at its commencement, it was equally so in the two centuries which have just been considered.

The history of the canon in the Syrian church cannot be traced with much exactness.

The Peshito version had only the Hebrew canonical books at first; most of the apocryphal were rendered from the Greek and added in the Nestorian recension. In the New Testament it wanted four of the catholic epistles and the Apocalypse. Ephrem (A.D. 378) uses all the books in our canon, the apocryphal as well as the canonical. The former are cited by him in the same way as the latter. Sirach ii. 1 is quoted with *as the Scripture says;*[1] and Wisdom iv. 7 with *it is written.*[2] Daniel xiii. 9, belonging to the Greek additions, is also cited with *as it is written.*[3] It should be observed that the quotations given are all from Ephrem's Greek, not Syriac, works; and that suspicions have been raised about the former being tampered with. The Syrian version of the New Testament made by Polycarp at the request of Philoxenus of Mabug, had the four

[1] *Opp. Græc.*, tom. ii. p. 327, ed. Rom. 1746.
[2] *Ibid.*, tom. i. p. 101   [3] Tom. iii. p. 60.

catholic epistles wanting in the Peshito. It had also the two epistles of Clement to the Corinthians, if we may judge by the Harclean recension, A.D. 616; for a MS. in the Cambridge University Library contains those epistles immediately after the Catholic ones, and before those of St Paul; so that they are put on an equality with the canonical writings. The Apocalypse is wanting. Junilius, (though an African bishop about 550 A.D.), says that he got his knowledge from a Persian of the name of Paulus who received his education in the school of Nisibis. He may, therefore, be considered a witness of the opinions of the Syrian church at the beginning of the 6th century. Dividing the biblical books into those of *perfect*, those of *intermediate*, and those of *no authority*, he makes the first the canonical; the second, those added to them by many (plures); the third, all the rest. In the first list he puts Ecclesiasticus. Among the second he puts

1 and 2 Chronicles, Job, Ezra and Nehemiah, Judith, Esther, 1 and 2 Maccabees; and in the New Testament, James, 2 Peter, Jude, 2 and 3 John. He also says that the Apocalypse of John is much doubted by the Orientals. In the third list, *i.e.*, books of no authority added by some (quidam) to the canonical, are put Wisdom and Canticles.[1] The catalogue is confused, and erroneous at least in one respect, that Jerome is referred to, as sanctioning the division given of the Old Testament books; for neither he nor the Jews agree with it.

The canon of the Abyssinian church seems to have had at first all the books in the Septuagint, canonical and apocryphal together, little distinction being made between them. Along with the contents of the Greek Bible there were Enoch, 4 Esdras, the Ascension of Isaiah, the Jubilees, Asseneth, &c. That of the New Testa-

[1] Galland, xii. p. 79, &c.

ment agrees with the present Greek one. At a later period in the Arabic age a list was made and constituted the legal one for the use of the church, having been derived from the Jacobite canons of the apostles. This gives, in the Old Testament, the Pentateuch, Joshua, Judges, Ruth, Judith, Kings, Chronicles, Ezra and Nehemiah, Esther, Tobit, two books of Maccabees, Job, Psalms, five books of Solomon, minor and greater prophets. The Wisdom of Sirach (for teaching children) and the book of Joseph ben Gorion, *i.e.*, that of the Maccabees, are external. The new Testament has four gospels, Acts, seven apostolic epistles, fourteen of Paul, and the Revelation of John. Later catalogues vary much, and are often enlarged with the book of Enoch, 4 Esdras, the Apocalypse of Isaiah, &c. The canon of the Ethiopic church was fluctuating.[1]

The canon of the Armenians had at first

[1] See Dillmann in Ewald's *Jahrbücher*, v. p. 144, &c.

the Palestinian books of the Old Testament, twenty-two in number, and the usual New Testament ones, except the Apocalypse. It was made from the Syriac in the fifth century by Sahak and Mesrob. The deutero-canonical books and additions were appended, after the disciples of those two men who had been sent by them into different places, brought back authentic copies of the Greek Bible from the patriarch Maximian, by which the version already made was interpolated and corrected; as it was subsequently corrected by others despatched to Alexandria and Athens, who, however, did not return till their teachers were dead. The MSS. of this version were afterwards interpolated from the Vulgate; Oskan himself translating for his edition (which was the first printed one, A.D. 1666), Sirach 4 Esdras and the Epistle of Jeremiah from the Latin. The book of Revelation does not seem to have been translated till the eighth century. Zohrab's critical edition (1805) has Judith, Tobit, the three books of Maccabees, Wisdom, and the Epistle of Baruch among the canonical books ; and in an appendix, the fourth book of Esdras, the prayer of Manasseh, the Epistle of the Corinthians to Paul and his answer, the Rest (end) of the apostle and evangelist John, the prayer of Euthalius. Like the edition of Oskan, this has all the deutero-canonical books, which were derived from the Septuagint, and incorporated by the first translators with their original version. Another edition published at St Petersburgh (1817), for the use of the Jacobite Church, has the prayer of Manasses and 4 Esdras after the Apocalypse.

The Georgian version consisted of the books and additions in the Greek translation from which it was made. The New Testament has the canonical books in the usual order. Jesus Sirach and two books of the Maccabees (2d and 3d) were not in the Georgian MS. used by Prince Arcil for the edition of 1743, but were rendered out of the Russian. The Moscow Bible printed under the direction and at the cost of Arcil, Bacchar and Wakuset, is the authorised edition of the Georgian Christians.

The Bible canon of the Eastern church in the middle ages shows no real advance. Endeavours were made to remove the uncertainty arising from the existence of numerous lists; but former decisions and decrees of councils were repeated instead of a new, independent canon. Here belongs the catalogue in the Alexandrian MS., of the fifth century, which is peculiar. After the prophets come Esther, Tobit, Judith, Ezra and Nehemiah, 4 Maccabees, Psalms, Job, Proverbs, Ecclesiastes, Canticles, the all-virtuous Wisdom, the Wisdom of Jesus of Sirach. In the New Testament, the Apocalypse is followed by two epistles of

Clement. The list was probably made in Egypt. That of Anastasius Sinaita,[1] patriarch of Antioch, is similar to Nicephorus's Stichometry, which we shall mention afterwards. Baruch is among the canonical books; Esther among the antilegomena. The Apocalypse is unnoticed. The 85th of the Apostolic canons gives a list of the Old and New Testament books, in which the usual canonical ones of the former are supplemented by Judith and 3 Maccabees; those of the latter by the two epistles of Clement, with the Apostolic constitutions. This catalogue cannot be put earlier than the fifth or sixth century, and is subject to the suspicion of having been interpolated. We have also Nicephorus's *Stichometry* (806-815;)[2] of which we may remark that Baruch is among the canonical books of the O. T.; while the Revelation is put with the Apocalypse of Peter,

[1] † 599 A.D.
[2] See Credner's *Zur. Gesch. des Kanons*, p. 97, &c.

the epistle of Barnabas and the Gospel according to the Hebrews, among the antilegomena of the N. T. It is also surprising that the Apocalypse of Peter and the Gospel according to the Hebrews are not among the Apocrypha, where Clement's epistles with the productions of Ignatius, Polycarp, and Hermas appear. The list is probably older than that of the Antioch patriarch Anastasius Sinaita. Cosmas Indicopleustes (535) never mentions the seven Catholic epistles of the New Testament or the Apocalypse. The Trullan council (A.D. 692) adopts the eighty-five Apostolic canons, rejecting, however, the Apostolic Constitutions. Photius, patriarch of Constantinople,[1] follows the eighty-fifth Apostolical canon, of the Trullan Council.[2] But in his Bibliotheca [3] he speaks differently regarding the epistles of

[1] † 891.
[2] *Nomocanon, Titulus III.*, cap. 2, vol. iv., pp. 1050, 1051 ed. Migne.
[3] See Codd. 113, 126.

Clement, and does not treat them as canonical. Though the first was thought worthy to be read in public, the second was rejected as spurious; and his own opinion was not altogether favourable to them. John of Damascus;[1] the second Nicene council (787); the Synopsis divinæ Scripturæ Vet. et Novi Test. (about 1000); Zonaras (about 1120); Alexius Aristenus (about 1160); and Nicephorus Callistus (1330), call for no remark.

In the Western church of the Middle Ages, diversity of opinion respecting certain books continued. Though the views of Augustine were generally followed, the stricter ones of Jerome found many adherents. The canon was fluctuating, and the practice of the churches in regard to it somewhat lax. Here belong Cassiodorus (about 550); the list in the Codex Amiatinus (about 550); Isidore of Seville[2] who, after enumerating three classes of Old Testa-

[1] † 754 A.D.   [2] † 636 A.D.

ment books gives a fourth not in the Hebrew canon. Here he specifies Wisdom, Ecclesiasticus, Tobit, Judith, 1 and 2 Maccabees, saying that the church of Christ puts them among the divine books, honours and highly esteems them.[1] There are also the fourth council of Toledo (632); Gregory the Great;[2] Notker Labeo;[3] Ivo (about 1092); Bede;[4] Alcuin;[5] Rabanus Maurus;[6] Hugo de St Victor;[7] Peter of Clugny;[8] John of Salisbury;[9] Thomas Aquinas;[10] Hugo de St Cher;[11] Wycliffe;[12] Nicolaus of Lyra,[13] &c., &c. Several of these, as Hugo de St Victor, John of Salisbury, Hugo de St Cher, and Nicolaus of Lyra, followed Jerome in separating the canonical and apocryphal books of the Old Testament.[14]

The Reformers generally returned to the

[1] *Etymolog.* vi. 1.   [2] †604 A.D.   [3] †912 A.D.
[4] †735 A.D.   [5] †804 A.D.   [6] †856 A.D.
[7] †1141 A.D.   [8] †1156 A.D.   [9] †1182 A.D.
[10] 1270 A.D.   [11] †1263 A.D.   [12] †1384 A.D.
[13] †1340 A.D.   [14] See Hody, p. 648, &c.

Hebrew canon, dividing off the additional books of the Septuagint or those attached to the Vulgate. These they called *apocryphal*, after Jerome's example. Though considered of no authority in matters of doctrine, they were pronounced useful and edifying. The principal reason that weighed with the Reformers was, that Christ and the apostles testified to none of the Septuagint additions.

Besides the canonical books of the Old Testament, Luther translated Judith, Wisdom, Tobit, Sirach, Baruch, 1 and 2 Maccabees, the Greek additions to Esther and Daniel, with the Prayer of Manasseh. His judgment respecting several of these is expressed in the prefaces to them. With regard to 1 Maccabees he thinks it almost equal to the other books of Holy Scripture, and not unworthy to be reckoned among them. Of Wisdom, he says, he was long in doubt whether it should be numbered among the canonical books; and of Sirach that it is a right good book proceeding from a wise man. But he speaks unfavourably of several other apocryphal productions, as of Baruch and 2 Maccabees. It is evident, however, that he considered all he translated of *some* use to the Christian Church. He thought that the book of Esther should not belong to the canon.

Luther's judgment respecting some of the New Testament books was freer than most Protestants now are disposed to approve. He thought the epistle to the Hebrews was neither Paul's nor an apostle's, but proceeded from an excellent and learned man who may have been the disciple of apostles. He did not put it on an equality with the epistles written by apostles themselves. The Apocalypse he considered neither apostolic nor prophetic, but put it almost on the same level with the 4th book of Esdras, which he spoke elsewhere of tossing into the Elbe. This judgment was afterwards modified, not retracted. James's epistle he pronounced unapostolic, "a right strawy epistle." In like manner, he did not believe that Jude's epistle proceeded from an apostle. Considering it to have been taken from 2 Peter, and not well extracted either, he put it lower than the supposed original. The Reformer, as also his successors, made a distinction between the books of the New Testament similar to that of the Old; the *generally received* (homologoumena) and *controverted* books (antilegomena); but the Calvinists afterwards obliterated it, as the Roman Catholics at the Council of Trent did with the old Testament.[1] The epistle to the Hebrews, those of Jude and James, with the Apocalypse, belong to the latter class. The distinction in question proceeded from genuine critical tact on the part of the early Lutheran Church which had canonical and deutero-canonical

---

[1] Chemnitz calls seven books of the New Testament *apocryphos*, because of their uncertain authorship (see *Examen Concilii Tridentini*, p. 45, &c.)

writings even in the New Testament collection. Nor did the Reformers consider it a dangerous thing to bring the fact before the people. To make it palpable, Luther attached continuous numbers to the first twenty-three books of his version, bringing the four antilegomena after these, without numbers; and this mode of marking the difference continued till the middle of the 17th century.[1] Luther was right in assigning a greater or less value to the separate writings of the New Testament, and in leaving every one to do the same. He relied on their internal value more than tradition; taking the *word of God* in a deeper and wider sense than its coincidence with the Bible.

Bodenstein of Carlstad examined the question of canonicity more thoroughly than any of his contemporaries, and followed out the principle of private judgment in regard to it. He divides

[1] See Tholuck's *Kommentar zum Briefe an die Hebräer, zweite Auflage*, pp. 55, 86.

the biblical books into three classes—1. Books of the highest dignity, viz., the Pentateuch and the Gospels; 2. Books of the second dignity, *i.e.*, the works termed prophetic by the Jews, and the fifteen epistles universally received; 3. Books of the third and lowest authority, *i.e.*, the Jewish Hagiographa and the seven Antilegomena epistles of the New Testament. Among the Apocrypha he makes two classes— such as are out of the canon to the Hebrews yet hagiographical (Wisdom, Ecclesiasticus, Judith, Tobit, the two Maccabees), and those that are clearly apocryphal and to be rejected (third and fourth Esdras, Baruch, Prayer of Manasseh, a good part of the third chapter of Daniel, and the last two chapters of Daniel.[1]

Zwingli asserts that the Apocalypse is not a biblical book.[2]

---

[1] Carlstadt's treatise is reprinted in Credner's *Zur Geschichte des Kanons*.

[2] *Werke*, edited by Schuler and Schulthess, vol. ii. p. 169.

Oecolampadius says—"We do not despise Judith, Tobit, Ecclesiasticus, Baruch, the last two Esdras, the three Maccabees, the last two chapters of Daniel, but we do not attribute to them divine authority with those others."[1] As to the books of the New Testament he would not compare the Apocalypse, James, Jude, 2 Peter, 2 and 3 John with the rest.[2]

Calvin did not think that Paul was the author of the epistle to the Hebrews, or that 2 Peter was written by the apostle himself; but both in his opinion are canonical.

[1] *Ep. ad. Valdenses* 1530, *apud Sculteti annal. evang. renovat decas secunda*, pp. 313, 314.

[2] *Ibid.*

CHAPTER VIII.

ORDER OF THE NEW TESTAMENT BOOKS.

I. THE arrangement of the various parts comprising the New Testament was fluctuating in the second century; less so in the third. In the fourth century the order which the books had commonly assumed in Greek MSS. and writers was: the Gospels, the Acts, the Catholic Epistles, the Pauline, and the Apocalypse. This sequence appears in the Vatican, Sinaitic, Alexandrian and Ephrem (C) MSS.; Cyril of Jerusalem, in the 60th Canon of the Laodicean Council, Athanasius, Leontius of Byzantium, &c.

II. Another order prevailed in the Latin Church, viz., the Gospels, the Acts, the Epistles of Paul, the Catholic Epistles, and the Apocalypse. This appears in Melito, Irenaeus, Clement of Alexandria, Origen, Augustine, Jerome, the Vulgate, the Councils of Carthage held in A.D. 397 and 419; and is now the usual arrangement.

Within the limits of the two general arrangements just mentioned, there were many variations. Thus we find in relation to *the gospels*.

III. (*a*) Matthew, John, Luke, Mark; in the MSS. of the old Italic marked *a, b, d, e, f, ff*, and in the cod. argenteus of Ulfila's Gothic version.

(*b*) Matthew, John, Mark, Luke; in the council of Ephesus A.D. 431, Cyril of Alexandria, Theodoret, the stichometry of the Clermont MS. Such was the usual order in the Greek Church of the fifth century.

(*c*) Mark is put first, followed by Matthew; in the fragment of a Bobbian MS. of the Itala at Turin marked *k*.

(*d*) Matthew, Mark, John, Luke; in the

Curetonian Syriac gospels. They are mentioned in the same order in Origen's I. Homily on Luke.

The reason of the order in (*a*) and (*b*) lies in apostleship. The works of apostles precede those of evangelists. The established sequence, which is already sanctioned by Irenæus and Origen, has respect to the supposed dates of the gospels. Clement of Alexandria says that ancient tradition supposed those gospels having the genealogies to have been written before the others.

IV. As to *the Acts of the Apostles*, not only is this work put immediately after the gospels, which is the order in the Muratorian canon, but we find it in other positions.

(*a*) Gospels, Pauline Epistles, Acts; in the Sinaitic MS., the Peshito,[1] Jerome,[2] and Epiphanius.

[1] Hug says that his copy of Widmanstad's edition had the Acts immediately following the Gospels.

[2] Epist. ad Paulinum.

(b) Gospels, Pauline Epistles, Catholic Epistles, Acts; in Augustine, the third council of Toledo, Isidore, Innocent I., Eugenius IV., and the Spanish Church generally.

(c) Gospels, Pauline, Catholic Epistles, Apocalypse, Acts; in the stichometry of the Clermont MS.

V. As to *the Epistles of Paul*, besides the place they now occupy in our Bibles, they sometimes follow the gospels immediately.

(a) Gospels, Pauline Epistles; the Sinaitic MS., Jerome, Epiphanius, Augustine, the third council of Toledo, Isidore, Innocent I., Eugenius IV., the stichometry of the Clermont MS.

(b) The usual order of the Greek Church is, Gospels, Acts, Catholic Epistles, Pauline, &c., as in Cyril of Jerusalem, the Laodicean Council (60), Athanasius, Leontius of Byzantium, the MSS. A. B., but not א. The critical Greek Testaments of Lachmann and Tischendorf adopt this order.

(*c*) They are placed last of all in a homily attributed to Origen, but this does not necessarily shew that father's opinion.[1]

(*d*) They stand first of all in a Gallican *Sacramentarium* cited by Hody.[2]

VI. With respect to the order of the individual epistles, the current one has been thought as old as Tertullian and Clement of Alexandria. But the proof of this is precarious. It appears in the fourth century, and may have been prior to that. It is in Epiphanius, who supposes that the arrangement was the apostle's own. Not only was it the prevalent one in the Greek Church, but also in the Latin, as we see from the codex Amiatinus, and the Vulgate MSS. generally. It rests upon the extent of the epistles and the relative importance of the localities in which the believers addressed resided.

[1] Hom. vii. in Josua.
[2] De Bibliorum textibus originalibus, &c., p. 654.

(*a*) Marcion had but ten Pauline epistles in the following order: Galatians, 1 and 2 Corinthians, Romans, 1 and 2 Thessalonians, the Laodiceans (Ephesians), Colossians, Philemon, Philippians.

(*b*) 1 and 2 Corinthians, Ephesians, Philippians, Colossians, Galatians, 1 and 2 Thessalonians, Romans, Philemon, Titus, 1 and 2 Timothy, to the Laodiceans, the Alexandrians (the Epistle to the Hebrews); in the Muratorian canon.

(*c*) Romans, Corinthians, Galatians, Ephesians, Philippians, Thessalonians, Colossians, Timothy, Titus, Philemon, Hebrews; in Augustine, and several MSS. of the Vulgate in England.[1]

(*d*) Romans, Corinthians, Galatians, Thessalonians, Ephesians, Philippians, Colossians, Timothy, Titus, Philemon, Hebrews; in the so-called decree of Gelasius in the name of

[1] *Ibid.*, p. 664.

Hormisdas, in Labbe's text. But here different MSS. vary in regard to the position of the Thessalonian epistles.

VII. The Laodicean letter was inserted either before the pastoral epistles, as in several MSS. of the Vulgate in England; or before the Thessalonian epistles preceding them; or at the end of the Epistle to the Hebrews, as in a MS. of the Latin Bible at Lambeth. Its insertion in copies of the Vulgate was owing to the authority of Gregory the Great, who looked upon it as authentic.

VIII. The position of the Epistle to the Hebrews usually was either before the pastoral epistles, *i.e.*, immediately after those to the Thessalonians; or after the pastoral ones and Philemon. The former method was generally adopted in the Greek Church from the fourth century. The latter prevailed in the Latin Church from Augustine onward.

(*a*) Pauline epistles to churches (the last

being the second to the Thessalonians), Hebrews, Timothy, Titus, Philemon; in the MSS. ℵ, A. B. C. H., Athanasius, Epiphanius, Euthalius,[1] Theodoret. Jerome mentions it after the epistles of Paul to the seven churches as an eighth excluded by the majority, and proceeds to specify the pastoral ones. But Amphilochius and Ebedjesu the Syrian have the western order, viz., the following—

(*b*) Pauline Epistles, Hebrews (following immediately that to Philemon); in Augustine and the Vulgate version generally. It is so in the canons of the councils at Hippo and Carthage (A.D. 393 and 397), and in the MSS. D. and G., in Isidore of Spain, and the council of Trent.

IX. With respect to the order of the *Catholic Epistles*, which were not *all* adopted into the canon till the end of the fourth century; Euse-

---

[1] See Zacagni's *Collectanea monumentorum veterum Praefat*, p. lxxi., &c.

bius putting all except 1 John and 1 Peter among the *antilegomena;* while Jerome, and the council of Carthage (A.D. 397) admit them unreservedly; the usual order, viz., James, 1 and 2 Peter, John, Jude, prevailed in the Eastern Church. It is in the Peshito or old Syriac version, Eusebius, Cyril of Jerusalem, Epiphanius, the 60th of the Laodicean canons, Athanasius, Gregory of Nazianzus, Amphilochius, the stichometry of Nicephorus, the MSS. ℵ. A. B. C., and most Greek MS. But the 76th of the Apostolic canons has Peter, John, James and Jude. The canon, however, is comparatively late.

(*a*) Peter, John, Jude, James; in Philastrius of Brescia. If we may rely on Cassiodorus's account of Augustine, the African father followed the same arrangement.

(*b*) Peter, James, Jude, John; in Rufinus.

(*c*) Peter, John, James, Jude; in the councils of Carthage, A.D. 397, 419, Cassiodorus, and a Gallican Sacramentarium. The Vulgate and council of Trent follow this arrangement.

(*d*) John, Peter, Jude, James ; in the list given by Innocent I., and the third council of Toledo.

The Eastern church naturally set the Epistle of James, who was Bishop of Jerusalem, at the head of the others ; while the Western put Peter, the Bishop of Rome, in the same place.

X. The Revelation varied little in position.

(*a*) In the decree of Gelasius, according to its three recensions, the Revelation follows Paul's epistles, preceding those of John and the other Catholic ones.

(*b*) In D or the Clermont MS. it follows the *Catholic* epistles, and precedes the Acts ; which last is thrown to the end of all the books, as if it were an appendix to the writings of the apostles.[1]

[1] See Volkmar's *Anhang* to *Credner's Geschichte des N. T. Kanon*, p. 341, &c. ; and Hody *De Bibliorum textibus originalibus*, p. 644, &c.

CHAPTER IX.

SUMMARY OF THE SUBJECT.

(*a.*) In relation to the Old Testament, the prevailing tendency in the Greek Church was to follow the Palestinian canon. Different lists appeared from time to time in which the endeavour there to exclude apocryphal, *i.e.*, spurious works, was apparent. In addition to the *canonical*, a class of *ecclesiastical* books was judged fit for reading in the Church, — a class intermediate between the canonical and apocryphal. The distinction between the canonical and ecclesiastical writings appears in Cyril of Jerusalem, Athanasius, Epiphanius, &c. The Latin Church showed a disposition to elevate the ecclesiastical books of the Greek Church to the rank of the canonical, making the line between the two indistinct; as we see from the acts of the councils at Hippo and Carthage, in the end of the fourth and beginning of the fifth century, where Augustine's influence was predominant. But notwithstanding this deviation from the stricter method of the Greeks, learned men like Jerome adhered to the Palestinian canon, and even styled the ecclesiastical books *apocryphal*, transferring the epithet from one class to another. Hilary and Rufinus also followed the Greek usage.

During the sixth and following centuries, it cannot be said that the canon of the Greek Church was definitely closed, notwithstanding the decrees of councils and references to older authorities. Opinions still varied about certain books, such as Esther; though the Palestinian list was commonly followed. During the same period, the enlarged canon of the Alexandrian Jews, which went far to abolish the distinction between the canonical and deutero-canonical books, prevailed in the West, at least in practice; though some followed the shorter one, sanctioned as it had been by Jerome. As both lists existed, no complete or final settlement of the question was reached in the Latin Church. Neither in the East nor in the West was the canon of the Old Testament really closed; for though the stricter principle of separation prevailed in theory, it was not carried out in practice consistently or universally. The two men most influential about the canon were Jerome and Augustine; the one representing its Palestinian, the other its Alexandrian type. After them no legal or commanding voice fixed either, to the absolute exclusion of its rival.

(*b*.) The charge of Constantine to Eusebius to make out a list of writings for the use of the Church and its performance may be considered as that which first put the subject on a broad and permanent basis. Its consequences were important. If it cannot be called the completion or close of the New Testament canon, it determined it largely. Eusebius made a Greek Bible containing the usual books, except the Revelation. Though the historian of the church was not well fitted for the task, being deficient in critical ability and trammelled by tradition, he doubtless used his best judgment. Hence, about the year 337, the Constantinian Church received a Bible which had an influential origin. No binding authority indeed attached to the list of the Christian books it presented; but it had weight in the Greek Church. It did not prevent different opinions, nor deter individuals from dissent. Thus Athanasius, who disliked Eusebius and his party, issued a list of the sacred writings which included the Revelation. The canon of the Làodicean Council (A.D. 363) agreed with the Constantine one.

That variations still existed in the Eastern Church is shewn by the lists which vied with one another in precedence. The apostolic canons

adopted the seven general epistles, while the
apostolic constitutions excluded them. The
Alexandrian MS. added to the ordinary books
of the New Testament Clement's two epistles;
and Cosmas Indicopleustes omitted the general
epistles as well as the Apocalypse. At length
the Council of Constantinople, usually called
the *Trullan* (A.D. 692), laid down positions that
fixed the canon for the Greek Church. The
endeavour in it was to attain to a conclusion
which should unite East and West. This
council did not enumerate the separate books,
but referred to older authorities, to the
eighty-five canons of the apostles, the decrees of the synods of Laodicea, Ephesus,
Carthage, and others; to Athanasius, Gregory
of Nazianzus, Amphliochius of Iconium, Cyril
of Alexandria, Gennadius, &c. After the
fourth century there was a general desire to
fall back on apostolic times, to appeal to
the Church, to ascertain the opinion of

synods or assemblies; in a word, to rely on authority.

Less discrepancy and activity were manifested about the canon in the Western Church. Here the chief doubts were directed to the epistle to the Hebrews and the seven general ones. The former was early excluded, and continued to be so even in the time of Jerome. The latter were adopted much sooner. The impulse given by Constantine to determine the books of Scripture re-acted on the West, where the Church considered it its own privilege. Augustine's influence contributed much to the settlement of the question. The synods of Hippo (A.D. 393) and of Carthage (A.D. 397) received the epistle to the Hebrews and the seven general ones, thus fixing the New Testament canon as it now is. In 419 the African bishops, in the presence of a Papal delegate, repeated their former decision. After the West Goths joined the Catholic Church in the sixth century, the Romish and

Spanish Churches gave prominence to the fact of accepting both the Apocalypse and the epistle to the Hebrews. The canon of the West was now virtually closed; the fourth Council of Toledo (A.D. 632) at which Isidore was present, agreeing with the Augustinian list, ratified as that list had been by Innocent the First. The reception of the epistle to the Hebrews was facilitated by the objections of the Arians and Semiarians; while opposition to the Priscillianists in Spain strengthened adherence to the traditional canon. Augustine and the Trullan Council fixed the number of the New Testament books as they are now.

With regard to the Bible canon in general, we see that councils had weight when they enumerated the sacred books; that prominent teachers delivered their opinion on the subject with effect, and that tradition contributed to one result; but no general council closed the canon once for all, till that of Trent promulgated its decrees. This body, however, could only settle the subject for Romanists, since, while the right of private judgment is exercised, no corporation can declare some books inspired and others not, some authoritative in matters of faith, others not, without presumption. Though the present Bible canon rests upon the judgment of good and learned men of different times, it can never be finally or infallibly settled, because the critical powers of readers differ, and all do not accept church authority with unhesitating assent.

It is the way of men to defer unduly to the opinions expressed by synods and councils, especially if they be propounded dogmatically; to acquiesce in their decisions with facility rather than institute independent inquiry. This is exemplified in the history of the canon, where the fallibility of such bodies in determining canonicity is conspicuous. It is so in the general reception of the book of Esther, while the old poem, the Song of Songs, was called in question at the synod of Jamnia; in the omission of the Revelation from the canonical list by many belonging to the Greek Church, while the epistles to Timothy and Titus were received as St Paul's from the beginning almost universally.

CHAPTER X.

THE CANON IN THE CONFESSIONS OF DIFFERENT CHURCHES.

THE second Helvetic Confession (A.D. 1566) speaks of the apocryphal books of the Old Testament as those which the ancients wished to be read in the churches, but not as authoritative in matters of faith.[1]

The Gallic Confession (A.D. 1559) makes a distinction between canonical and other books, the former being the rule and norm of faith, not only by the consent of the Church, but much more by the testimony and intrinsic persuasion of the Spirit, by whose suggestions we are taught to distinguish them from other ecclesiastical books which, though useful, are not of the kind

---

[1] Niemeyer, *Collectio Confessionum*, p. 468.

that any article of faith can be constituted by them.[1]

The Belgic Confession (A.D. 1561) makes a distinction between the sacred and apocryphal books. The latter may be read by the Church, but no doctrine can be derived from them. In the list of New Testament books given there are *fourteen* epistles of Paul.[2]

The canon of the Waldenses must have coincided at first with that of the Roman Church; for the Dublin MS. containing the New Testament has attached to it the Book of Wisdom and the first twenty-three chapters of Sirach; while the Zurich codex of the New Testament has marginal references to the Apocrypha; to Judith, Tobit, 4 Esdras, Wisdom, Sirach, and Susanna. The *Nobla Leyczon* containing a brief narration of the contents of the Old and New Testaments confirms this opinion,

[1] Niemeyer's *Collectio Confessionum*, p. 330.
[2] *Ibid.*, pp. 361, 362.

It opposes, however, the old law to the new, making them antagonistic. The historical document containing the articles of "The Union of the Valleys," A.D. 1571, separates indeed the canonical and apocryphal books, purporting to be founded on a Confession of Faith as old as A.D. 1120; but the latter is mythical, as appears from a comparison of it with the epistle which the legates of the Waldensians gave to Œcolampadius. The articles of that "Union" are copied from Morel's account of his transactions with Œcolampadius and Bucer in 1530. The literature of this people was altered by Hussite influences and the Reformation; so that though differing little from the Romanists at first except in ecclesiastical discipline, they diverged widely afterwards by adopting the Protestant canon and doctrines.[1] Hence the Confession issued

[1] See Herzog's *Die Romanischen Waldenser*, p. 55, &c.; and his programm *De origine et pristino statu Waldensium*, &c., pp. 17, 40, 41.

in 1655 enumerates as Holy Scripture nothing but the Jewish Palestinian canon, and the usual books of the New Testament.[1]

The canon of the Anglican Church (1562), given in the sixth article of religion, defines holy Scripture to be "those canonical books of the Old and New Testament, of whose authority was never any doubt in the Church." After giving the names and number of the canonical books, the article prefaces the apocryphal ones with, "And the other books (as Hierome saith) the Church doth read for example of life and instruction of manners; but yet doth it not apply them to establish any doctrine. Such are these following," &c., &c. At the end it is stated that "all the books of the New Testament, as they are commonly received, we do receive and account them canonical." The article is ambiguous. If the canonical books enumerated are those meant in the phrase "of whose authority

[1] Leger's *Histoire des Eglises Vaudoises*, vol. i., p. 112, &c.

was never any doubt in the Church," the statement is incorrect. If a distinction is implied between the canonical books and such canonical ones as have never been doubted in the Church, the meaning is obscure. In either case the language is not explicit.

The Scottish or Westminster Confession of Faith gives a list of all the books of the Old and New Testaments as the Word of God written; adding that those called the apocrypha are not of divine inspiration, and no part of the canon,—of no authority in the Church, nor to be approved or made use of otherwise than human writings.

The Roman Catholic canon was finally determined at the Council of Trent (1546), which adopted all the books in the Vulgate as sacred and canonical, without distinction. Third and fourth Esdras, third Maccabees, and the prayer of Manasseh were not included; though the first and last appeared in the original

Clementine edition of 1592, but apart from the canonical books. They are not in the Sixtine edition of 1590.[1] A council at Florence in 1441 had set the example which was followed at Trent. But this stringent decree did not prevent individual Catholics from making a distinction between the books, in assuming a first and second canon or proto-canonical and deutero-canonical books; as did Sixtus Senensis, B. Lamy, Anton a matre Dei, Jahn, and others; though it is hardly consistent with orthodox Catholicism or the view of those who passed the decree. When the writings are said to be of different authority—some more, others less—the intent of the council is violated. The Vatican council (1870) confirmed the Tridentine decree respecting the canon.

The Greek Church, after several ineffectual

[1] The reason given for their being added as a separate appendix is that they are cited by some fathers and found in some Latin Bibles.

attempts to uphold the old distinction between the canonical and ecclesiastical books by Metrophanes Critopulus patriarch of Alexandria in 1625, and Cyril Lucaris patriarch of Constantinople (1638 A.D.),[1] came to the same decision with the Romish, and canonized all the apocrypha. This was done at a Jerusalem synod under Dositheus in 1672.

[1] Kimmel's *Monumenta fidei eccles. orient*, part i. p. 467.

CHAPTER XI.

THE CANON FROM SEMLER TO THE PRESENT TIME, WITH REFLECTIONS ON ITS READJUSTMENT.

SEMLER [1] was the most conspicuous scholar after the Reformation who undertook to correct the prevailing ideas respecting the canon. Acquainted with the works of Toland and Morgan, he adopted some of their views, and prosecuted his inquiries on their lines chiefly in relation to the New Testament. He had no definite principles to guide him, but judged books chiefly by their christian value and use to the Church. Though his views are sometimes one-sided and his essays ill-digested, he placed the subject in new lights, and rendered a service

[1] †1791 A D.

to truth which bore abundant fruit in after years.[1] He dealt tradition severe blows, and freed theology from the yoke of the letter. He was followed by his disciple Corrodi, by G. L. Oeder, J. D. Michaelis, Herder, Lessing, and Eichhorn, —most of whom recommended their views by a freshness of style which Semler did not command. The more recent works of Gesenius, De Wette, Zunz, Ewald, Hitzig, Geiger and Herzfeld have contributed to form a juster opinion of the true position which the books of the Bible occupy.

In the New Testament, the writings of F. C. Baur have opened up a new method of investigating the canon, which promises important and lasting results. Proceeding in the track of Semler, he prosecuted his researches into primitive Christianity with great acuteness and singular power of combination. Though his

---

[1] *Abhandlung von freier Untersuchung des Canon*, 4 parts, Halle, 1771-1775.

separation of Petrine and Pauline christianity is not new, he has applied it in ways which neither Toland nor Morgan was competent to manage. These writers perceived the difference between the leading principle of the twelve and that of Paul, they had some far-seeing glimpses of the origin and differences of the New Testament writings,[1] but they propounded them in an unsystematic way along with untenable conjectures. It was reserved for the Tübingen professor to elaborate the hypothesis of an Ebionite or primitive christianity in contra-distinction from a Pauline, applying it to the origin and constitution of christian literature; in a word, to use a *tendenz-kritik* for opening up the genius of the sacred writings as well as the stages of early christianity out of which they arose. The head of the Tübingen school, it is true, has carried out the antagonism between

[1] See Toland's *Nazarenus*, p. 25, &c., second edition; and Morgan's *Moral Philosopher*, vol. i. p. 56, &c.

the Petrine and Pauline christians too rigorously, and invaded the authenticity of the sacred writings to excess; for it is hazardous to make a theory extremely stringent to the comparative neglect of modifying circumstances, which, though increasing the difficulty of criticism, contribute to the security of its processes. Yet he has properly emphasized internal evidence; and many of his conclusions about the books will stand. He has thrown much light on the original relations of parties immediately after the origin of Christianity, and disturbed an organic unity of the New Testament which had been merely *assumed* by traditionalists. The best Introductions to the New Testament must accept them to some extent. The chief characteristic of the school is the application of historic criticism to the genesis of the New Testament writings, irrespective of tradition— a striving to discover the circumstances or tendencies out of which the books originated.

Baur's *tendenz* - principle judiciously applied cannot but produce good results.

We have seen that sound critical considerations did not regulate the formation of the three collections which make up the entire canon of the Old Testament. Had it been so, the Pentateuch would not have been attributed to Moses. Neither would a number of latter prophecies have been accepted as Isaiah's and incorporated with the prophet's authentic productions. All the Proverbs, the book of Ecclesiastes, and the Song of Songs would not have been assigned to Solomon; Jonah would have been separated from the prophets, and Daniel must have had a later position in the Hagiographa. We cannot, therefore, credit the collectors or editors of the books with great critical sagacity. But they did their best in the circumstances, preserving invaluable records of the Hebrew people. In like manner, it has appeared, that the ecclesiastics to whom we owe the New Testament collection were not sharp-sighted in the literature with which they had to do. It is true that well-founded doubts were entertained by the early Christians about several portions, such as the second Epistle of Peter, the Epistle to the Hebrews, &c., but the Revelation was needlessly discredited. They accepted without hesitation the pastoral epistles as Pauline, but doubted some of the Catholic Epistles, whch bear the impress of authenticity more strongly, such as James. It is therefore incorrect to say that 2 Peter, 2 and 3 John, James, Jude, Epistle to the Hebrews, and the Apocalypse "have been received into the canon on evidence less complete" than that belonging to the others. The very general admission of the fourth gospel as the apostle John's, is a curious example of facile traditionalism. Biblical criticism, however, scarcely existed in the first three centuries. It is for us to set the subject in another light, because our means of judging are superior. If the resources of the early fathers were inadequate to the proper sifting of a copious literature, they should be mildly judged.

The question of the canon is not settled. It is probably the work of successive inquirers to set it on a right basis, and adjust the various parts in a manner consistent with historic criticism, sound reason, and religion. The absolute and relative worth of books; the degrees in which they regulate ethics and conduct; their varying values at the times of their first appearance and our own; their places in the general history of human progress,—all these must be determined before the documents of Judaism and Christianity be classified aright. Their present arrangement is external. Based on no interior principle, it furnishes little help toward a thorough investigation of the whole. Those who look upon the question as historical and literary take a one-sided view. It has a theological character also. It needs the application, not only of historic criticism, but the immediate consciousness belonging to every Christian. The two Testaments should be separated, and their respective positions assigned to each—the Old having been preparatory to the New. Should it be said bluntly, as it is in the 7th Article of the Anglican Church, that the Old is not contrary to the New Testament? Luther at least expressed his opinion of the difference between them pretty clearly;[1] though the theologians of Germany after him evinced a desire to minimise the difference.[2] Should the general opinion of

[1] For example, "Moses is dead; his rule went out when Christ came—he is of no further service here. . . . We are willing to regard him as a teacher, but we will not regard him as our lawgiver, *unless he agree with the New Testament and the law of nature.*" *Sämmtliche Schriften*, ed. Walch. dritter Theil., pp. 7, 8.

[2] Such as Calovius, Chemnitz, John Gerhard, W. Lyser, Quenstedt, Brochmand, Hollaz, &c. Melancthon also makes

the Protestant Church that the authority of the Old Testament is not subordinate to that of the New be rigidly upheld? According to one aspect of the former it may be so, viz., its prophetic and theological aspect, that in which it is brought into close union with the latter; the essence of the one being foreshadowed or implied in the other, as Justin Martyr supposed. And this view has never lost supporters, who by the help of double senses, types, and symbols, with assumed prediction of the definite and distant future, transform the old dispensation into an outline picture of the new; taking into it a body of divinity which is alien from its nature. According to another aspect, viz., the moral and historical, the equality can scarcely be allowed. Schleiermacher is right in saying that the Old Testament seems to be nothing but a superfluous authority for doctrine; an

no important distinction between the two Testaments in his *Loci theologici*. Calvin's theology was derived from the Old Testament more than the New.

opinion coinciding with that of the early Socinians, who held that it has a historical, not a dogmatic, value. Only such of our pious emotions as are of a general nature are accurately reflected in the Old Testament; and all that is most decidedly Jewish is of least value to christians. The alleged coincidence of the Old Testament with the New must be modified by the doctrine of development. It has been fostered by types and prophecies supposed to refer to christian times; by the assumed *dictation* of all Scripture by the Holy Spirit; by fancied references of the one dispensation to the other; by the confounding of a Jewish Messiah sketched in various prophets, with Jesus Christ, as if the latter had not changed, exalted and purified the Messianic idea to suit his sublime purposes of human regeneration. The times and circumstances in which the Old Testament Scriptures appeared, the manners, usages, civilisation, intellectual and moral stage of the

Semitic race combine to give them a lower position than that of the New Testament books which arose out of a more developed perception of the relations between God and men. Spiritual apprehension had got beyond Jewish particularism, especially in the case of the apostle Paul, who gave the new religion a distinct vitality by severing it from its Jewish predecessor.

The agreement of the New Testament books with themselves must be modified by the same doctrine of development. Jewish and Pauline christianity appear in different works, necessarily imparting a difference of views and expression; or they are blended in various degrees, as in the epistles to the Hebrews and the first of Peter. Hence absolute harmony cannot be looked for. If the standpoints of the writers were so diverse, how can their productions coincide? The alleged coincidence can only be intersected with varieties proportioned to the measures in which

the authors possessed the Spirit of God. These
varieties affect the matter as well as the manner
of the writings. It is therefore unphilosophical
to treat the Bible as a whole which was dictated
by the Spirit and directed to one end. Its
uniformity is chequered with variety; its harmony with disagreement. It is a bundle of
books; a selection from a wider literature,
reflecting many diversities of religious apprehension. After the two Testaments have been
rightly estimated according to their respective
merits, the contents of each should be duly
apportioned—internal evidence being the test of
their relative importance, irrespective of *a priori*
assumptions. Their traditional origin and
authority must be subordinated to the inherent
value they bear, or the conformity of the ideas
to the will of God. The gradual formation of
both canons suggests an analysis of the classes
into which they came to be put; for the same
canonical dignity was not attributed by the

Jews to the books contained in the three divisions; and the controverted writings of the New Testament found gradual recognition very slowly. Luther made important distinctions between the canonical books[1]; and Carlstadt put the Antilegomena of the New Testament on a par with the Hagiographa of the Old.

In the Old Testament the three classes or canons have been generally estimated by the Jews according to their respective antiquity; though the sacrificial worship enjoined in the Pentateuch never formed an essential part of the Jewish religion; the best prophets having set small value upon it. The pure monotheistic doctrine of these last writers, chiefly contained in the second canon, lifts that class up to the highest rank; yet the Decalogue in the Penta-

---

[1] His full sayings are collected in Bretschneider's *Luther an unsere Zeit*, pp. 186-224; and in Krause's *Opuscula theologica*, pp. 205-241.

teuch is sufficient to stamp the first canon with great worth. It must be confessed, however, that the Mosaic law was meagre, in the domain of pure ethics; and that it promoted among the people a slavish spirit of positivism by laying more stress on acts than dispositions, and insisting on small regulations. For this reason, the prophets combated its narrow externality. The three canons were regarded with a degree of veneration corresponding to the order in which they stand. To apportion their respective values to the individual parts of them is a difficult task.

As to the New Testament writings, we think that some of them might conveniently occupy the position of *duetero-canonical*, equivalent to those of the Old Testament having that title. We allude to 2 and 3 John, Jude, James, 2 Peter, the Revelation. It is true that a few of these were prior in time to some of the universally-received gospels or epistles; but time is not an important factor in a good classification. Among the Pauline epistles themselves, classification might be adopted; for the pastoral letters are undoubtedly post-Pauline, and inferior to the authentic ones. In classifying the New Testament writings, three things might be considered—the reception they met with from the first, their authenticity, above all, their internal excellence. The subject is not easy, because critics are not universally agreed about the proper rank and authenticity of a few documents. The Epistle to the Colossians, for example, creates perplexity; that to the Ephesians is less embarrassing, its post-Pauline origin being tolerably clear.

What is wanted is a rational historic criticism to moderate the theological hypotheses with which the older Protestants set out, the supernatural inspiration of the books, their internal inseparability, and their direct reference to the work of salvation. It must be allowed that

many points are independent of dogmatics;
and that the right decision in things historical
may be reached apart from any ecclesiastical
standpoint.

Again, should the distinction between the
apocryphal and canonical books of the Old
Testament be emphasized as it is by many?
Should a sharp line be put between the two,
as though the one class, with the period it
belonged to, were characterized by the errors
and anachronisms of its history; the other by
simplicity and accuracy; the one, by books
written under fictitious names; the other, by
the power to distinguish truth from falsehood
or by honesty of purpose? Should the one
be a sign of the want of truthfulness and
discernment; the other, of religious simplicity?
Can this aggregation of the Apocrypha over
against the Hagiographa, serve the purpose
of a just estimate? Hardly so; for some of
the latter, such as Esther and Ecclesiastes,

cannot be put above Wisdom, 1st Maccabees, Judith, Baruch, or Ecclesiasticus. The doctrine of immortality, clearly expressed in the Book of Wisdom, is not in Ecclesiastes ; neither is God once named in the Book of Esther as author of the marvellous deliverances which the chosen people are said to have experienced. The history narrated in 1st Maccabees is more credible than that in Esther. It is therefore misleading to mark off all the apocryphal works as *human* and all the canonical ones as *divine*. The divine and the human elements in man are too intimately blended to admit of such separation. The best which he produces partakes of both. The human element still permeates them as long as God speaks through man; and He neither dictates nor speaks otherwise. In the attributes claimed for the canonical books no rigid line can be drawn. It may be that the inspiration of their authors differed in degree; that the writer of Ecclesiastes, for example, was more philosophical than Jesus son of Sirach; but different degrees of inspiration belong to the canonical writers themselves. Undue exaltation of the Hebrew canon does injustice to the wider Alexandrian one. Yet some still speak of "the pure Hebrew canon," identifying it with that of the Church of England. We admit that history had become legendary, that it was written in an oratorical style by the Alexandrian Jews, and was used for didactic purposes as in Tobit and Judith. Gnomic poetry had survived in the book of Sirach; prophecy, in Baruch and the Epistle of Jeremiah, though here the language is already prosaic. Imitation is too observable in the matter and manner of the Apocrypha. They have parallels, however, among the Hagiographa, which originated in an age when the genuine breath of prophetic inspiration had ceased; when history and prophecy had degenerated; so that the transition from Esther and

Malachi to Judith and Baruch, as also from Proverbs to Wisdom, is not great.

The *Talmudic* canon is generally adopted at the present day. It was not, however, universally received even by the Jews; for Esther was omitted out of it by those from whom Melito got his catalogue in Palestine; while Sirach was annexed to it as late as the beginning of the 4th century. Baruch was also added in several Jewish circles, doubtless on account of its supposed authorship. Thus "the pure Hebrew canon" was not one and the same among all Jews; and therefore the phrase is misleading. Neither is it correct to say that it is the only canon distinctly recognized during the first four centuries, unless the usage of the early fathers be set over against their *assumed* contrary judgment; nor can all who followed the Alexandrian canon be pronounced uncritical, including Origen himself. A stereotyped canon of the Old Testament, either among Jews or

Christians of the first four centuries, which excluded all the apocryphal books and included all the canonical ones, cannot be shown. And in regard to "the critical judgment" of Jews and Christians in that period it is arbitrary to suppose that such as adopted the present canonical books alone were more discerning than others. They were more traditional and conservative; their discriminating faculty not corresponding to the degree of their reliance on the past.

The aim of the inquirer should be to find from competent witnesses—from contemporaneous or succeeding writers of trustworthy character—the authors and ages of the biblical books. When evidence of this kind is not available as often happens, the only resource is the internal. The external evidence in favour of the canon is all but exhausted, and nothing of importance can be added to it now. Its strength has been brought out; its weakness has not been equally exhibited. The problem resolves itself into an examination of internal characteristics, which may be strong enough to modify or counterbalance the external. The latter have had an artificial preponderance in the past; henceforward they must be regulated by the internal. The main conclusion should be drawn from the contents of the books themselves. And the example of Jews and Christians, to whom we owe the Bible canon, shows that *classification* is necessary. This is admitted both by Roman Catholic writers and orthodox Protestants. A gloss-writer on what is usually called the "decree of Gratian," *i.e.*, the Bolognese canonist of the 12th century, remarks about the canonical books, "all may be received but may not be held in the same estimation." John Gerhard speaks of a *second order*, containing the books of the New Testament, about whose authors there were some doubts in the Church;[1]

[1] *Loci Theologici*, Tom. i. pp. 186, 187, ed. Cotta, 1762.

and Quenstedt similarly specifies *proto-canonical* and *deutero-canonical* New Testament books, or those of the first and second order.[1] What are degrees or kinds of inspiration assumed by many, but a tacit acknowledgment of the fact that books vary in intrinsic value as they are more or less impregnated with divine truth or differ in the proportion of the eternal and temporal elements which commingle in every revealed religion? Doubtless the authors from whom the separate books proceeded, if discoverable, should be regarded; the inspiration of an Isaiah is higher than that of a Malachi, and an apostle is more authoritative than an evangelist; but the authors are often unknown. Besides, the process of redaction through which many of the writings passed hinders an exact knowledge of authorship. In these circumstances the books themselves must determine the position they should occupy

[1] *Theologia Didactico-polemica*, p. 340.

in the estimation of those who are looking at records of the past to help their spiritual life. And if it be asked, What principle should lie at the basis of a thorough classification? the answer is, the *normative element* contained in the sacred books. This is the characteristic which should regulate classification. The time when a book appeared, its author, the surrounding circumstances that influenced him, are of less consequence than its bearing upon the spiritual education of mankind. The extent of its adequacy to promote this end determines the rank. Such books as embody the indestructible essence of religion with the fewest accidents of time, place and nature—which present conditions not easily disengaged from the imperishable life of the soul, deserve the first rank. Whatever Scriptures express ideas consonant with the nature of God as a holy, loving, just and good Being—as a benevolent Father not willing the destruction of any of his children; the Scriptures presenting ideas of Him consistent with pure reason and man's highest instincts, besides such as set forth our sense of dependence on the infinite; the books, in short, that contain a revelation from God with least admixture of the human conditions under which it is transmitted—these belong to the highest class. If they lead the reader away from opinion to practice, from dogma to life, from non-doing to obedience to the law of moral duty, from the notion that everything in salvation has been done for him to the keeping of the commandments, from particularist conceptions about the divine mercy to the widest belief of its overshadowing presence—such books of Scripture are in that same proportion to be ranked among the best. In regard to the Old Testament, conformity to Christ's teaching will determine rank; or, which is tantamount, conformity to that pure reason which is God's natural revelation in man; a criterion which assigns various ranks to such Scriptures as appeared among a Semite race at a certain stage of its development. In the New Testament, the words and precepts of Jesus have a character of their own, though it is very difficult to select them from the gospels. The supposition that the apostles' productions possess a higher authority than those of their disciples, is natural. But the immediate followers of Christ did not all stand on one platform. Differing from one another even in important principles, it is possible, if not certain, that some of their disciples' composition may be of higher value. The spirit of God may have wrought within the apostles generally with greater power and clearness than in other teachers; but its operation is conditioned not merely by outward factors but by individual idiosyncracy; so that one who had not seen the Lord and was therefore not an apostle proper, may have apprehended his mind better than an immediate disciple. Paul stood above the primitive apostles in the extent to which he fathomed the pregnant sayings of Jesus and developed their latent germs. Thus the normative element—that which determines the varying degrees of authority belonging to the New Testament—does not lie in apostolic authorship but internal worth; in the clearness and power with which the divine Spirit enabled men to grasp the truth. By distinguishing the *temporal* and the *eternal* in christianity, the writings necessarily rise or sink in proportion to these elements. The *eternal* is the essence and gem of revealed truth. Perfectibility belongs only to the *temporal;* it cannot be predicated of the *eternal.*

The multitudinous collection of books contained in the Bible is not pervaded by unity of purpose or plan, so as to make a good classification easy. Least of all is it dominated by such substantial unity as has been connected with one man; for the conception of a Messiah was never the national belief of Judaism, but a notion projected by prophets into the future to comfort the people in times of disaster; the forecasting of aspirations doomed to disappointment. From the collection presenting various degrees of intellectual and moral development, it is difficult to see a sufficient reason for some being canonised to the exclusion of better works which were relegated to the class of the *apocryphal*.

Mr Jones's[1] statement that the primitive Christians are proper judges to determine what book is canonical, requires great modification, being too vague to be serviceable; for "primitive Christians" is a phrase that needs to be defined. How far do they extend? How much of the first and second centuries do they cover? Were not the primitive Christians

[1] See Jones's new and full method of settling the canonical authority of the New Testament, Vol. I., Part i., chap. 5, page 52, ed. 1726.

divided in their beliefs? Did the Jewish and the Pauline ones unite in accepting the same writings? Not for a considerable time, until the means of ascertaining the real authors of the books and the ability to do so were lacking.

As to the Old Testament, the Palestinian Jews determined the canonical books by gradually contracting the list and stopping it at a time when their calamities throwing them back on the past for springs of hope, had stiffened them within a narrow traditionalism; but their brethren in Egypt, touched by Alexandrian culture and Greek philosophy, received later productions into their canon, some of which at least are of equal value with Palestinian ones. In any case, the degree of authority attaching to the Biblical books grew from less to greater, till it culminated in a divine character, a sacredness rising even to infallibility. Doubtless the Jews of Palestine distinguished the canonical from the apocryphal or deutero-canonical books on grounds satisfactory to themselves; but their judgment was not infallible. A senate of Rabbis under the old dispensation might err, as easily as a synod of priests under the new. Though they may have been *generally* correct, it must not be assumed that they were *always* so. Their discernment may be commended without being magnified. The general feeling of leaning upon the past was a sound one, for the best times of Judaism had departed, and with them the most original effusions; yet the wave of Platonism that passed over Alexandria could not but quicken even the conservative mind of the Jew. Greek thought blended with echoes of the past, though in dulled form. Still a line had to be drawn in the national literature; and it was well drawn on the whole. The feeling existed that the collection must be closed with works of a certain period and a certain character; and it was closed accordingly, without preventing individuals from putting their private opinions over against authority, and dissenting.

At the present day a new arrangement is necessary; but where is the ecclesiastical body bold enough to undertake it? And if it were attempted or carried out by non-ecclesiastical parties, would the churches approve or adopt the proceeding? We venture to say, that if some books be separated from the collection and others put in their place—if the classification of some be altered, and their authority raised or lowered—good will be done; the Bible will have a fairer degree of normal power in doctrine and morals, and continue to promote spiritual life. Faith in Christ precedes faith in books. Unless criticism be needlessly negative it cannot remove this time-honoured legacy from the position it is entitled to, else the spiritual consciousness of humanity will rebel. While the subject is treated reverently, and the love of truth overrides dogmatic prejudices, the canon will come forth in a different form from that which it has had for centuries—a form on which faith may rest without misgiving.

The canon was a work of divine providence, because history, in a religious view, necessarily implies the fact. It was a work of inspiration, because the agency of the Holy Spirit has always been with the people of God as a principle influencing their life. It was not, however, the result of a *special* or *peculiar* act of divine inspiration at any one time, but of a gradual illuminating process, shaped by influences more or less active in the divine economy.

The canonical authority of Scripture does not depend on any church or council. The early church may be cited as *a witness* for it; that is all. Canonical authority lies in Scripture itself, and is inherent in the books so far as they contain a declaration of the divine will. Hence there is truth in the statement of old theologians that the authority of Scripture is from God alone. It was the early church indeed that made the canon, selecting the books which appeared to have been written by apostles or apostolic men, and carrying over to them authority from alleged authenticity more than internal value. But the latter is the real index of authority; and God is the fountain from whom spiritual endowments proceed.[1] The *canonicity* of the books is a distinct question

---

[1] Ecclesia sua autoritate nullum librum facit canonicum, quippe canonica scripturae autoritas est a solo Deo, &c. Gerhard's *Loci Theologici*, tom. i. p. 4, ed. Cotta. Autoritas scripturæ quoad nos nihil aliud est, quam manifestatio et cognitio unicæ illius divinæ et summæ autoritatis, quæ scripturæ est interna et insita. Ecclesia igitur non confert scripturæ novam aliquam autoritatem quoad nos, sed testificatione sua ad agnitionem illius veritatis nos deducit. Concedimus, ecclesiam esse scripturæ sacræ *testem, custodem, vindicem, praeconem, et interpretem ;* sed negamus, ex eo effici, quod autoritas scripturæ sive simpliciter sive quoad nos ab ecclesia pendeat et quidem unice, pendeat.—*Ibid.*, tomus secundus, p. 39, ed. Cotta.

from that of their *authenticity*. The latter is a thing of historic criticism; the former of doctrinal belief. Their ecclesiastical authority rests on outward attestation; their normal, on faith and feeling.

www.ingramcontent.com/pod-product-compliance
Lightning Source LLC
Chambersburg PA
CBHW050339230426
43663CB00010B/1922